The Most Epic Soccer Stories for Kids

Discover incredible true stories from soccer legends that will inspire young athletes to dream big and shoot for the stars!

By

W. Bo Cricklewood

W. Bo Cricklewood

"Success is no accident. It is hard work, perseverance, learning, studying, sacrifice and most of all, love of what you are doing or learning to do."

-Pelé

W. Bo Cricklewood

Table of Contents

Introduction

Imagine this: The crowd roars as you sprint down the field, the ball at your feet. You weave past defenders, your heart pounding with every step. The goal is in sight. You take a deep breath, wind up, and unleash a powerful shot. The ball soars through the air, curving beautifully past the goalkeeper's outstretched hands. GOAL!

Welcome to "The Most Epic Soccer Stories for Kids," where dreams like these come to life. Get ready to dive into the incredible journeys of soccer's greatest legends. But here's the thing – these superstars didn't start out as champions. They were once kids just like you, with big dreams and even bigger challenges.

Did you know that Cristiano Ronaldo used to practice with wadded-up socks because he couldn't afford a real ball? Or that Lionel Messi honed his dribbling skills using oranges? These players turned obstacles into opportunities, and that's what this book is all about.

As you read these thrilling tales, you'll discover the secrets behind their success. It's not just about fancy footwork or powerful kicks. It's about never giving up, working together as a team, and believing in yourself even when things get tough.

So lace up your cleats and get ready for an adventure. These stories aren't just about soccer - they're about life. They'll show you how to turn your own challenges into victories, both on and off the field. Who knows? Maybe one day, we'll be reading about your epic soccer story!

W. Bo Cricklewood

Chapter 1: The Boy from Madeira: Cristiano Ronaldo's Rise from Poverty to Stardom

Humble Beginnings

In a small, charming village tucked away among the lush green hills of Madeira, Portugal, a young boy named Cristiano Ronaldo began his journey from humble beginnings. The world beyond his village was vast, alive with bright lights and cheering crowds, but for little Cristiano, soccer was just a tiny flicker on the horizon, barely noticeable amid the routines of daily life. His home was simple, filled with the comforting scents of home-cooked meals and the cheerful sounds of family laughter, yet there was a fire within him that hinted at something greater waiting to be unleashed.

Cristiano lived in a small apartment with his family, where every square inch was filled with love and dreams. While other kids had big backyards and fancy toys, Cristiano's playground was shaped by his imagination and resourcefulness. He crafted his favorite makeshift soccer ball from discarded materials, showing off his creativity. Using old socks wrapped tightly together and patched with whatever he could find, this was more than just a toy for him; it was a lifeline, a shining symbol of hope and ambition.

The streets became his arena, and with every kick, he discovered the basics of the beautiful game. While other kids played with shiny, new balls and the latest gear, Cristiano understood that it wasn't the equipment that made a great player; it was the heart and commitment behind every move. His love for soccer drove him to practice tirelessly, dribbling through narrow alleys and weaving between cobblestones, where every step felt like a dance, and every shot rang out with determination.

Though his family didn't have much money, they recognized how vital it was to support their son's dreams. His father, who worked as a kit man at a local soccer club, filled Cristiano's head with stories of legendary players. These tales painted vivid images in his mind, igniting his desire to follow in their footsteps and one day be among them. His mother, a strong and caring woman, reminded him that dreams are built on hard work, encouraging him to stay relentless in chasing them. The love and support from his family provided a solid foundation, allowing him to dream big, even when resources were limited.

Despite the lack of luxury, the environment in which he grew up helped shape his character. Each challenge became a lesson, and every setback pushed him to improve. Life in Madeira wasn't always easy; there were tough moments that could have crushed a lesser spirit. But Cristiano was different. The hardships he faced became a key part of who he was, teaching him resilience and determination that would set him apart as he moved forward.

He formed a close bond with friends who shared his passion for soccer. They would gather every afternoon to play on whatever patch of grass they could find, turning their dreams into reality with every goal scored. In those moments of laughter and teamwork, Cristiano first experienced the joy of camaraderie. The spirit of competition was alive, and the happiness of the game shone brightly on their faces. For these kids, soccer became a universal language, connecting them and helping them rise above their challenges.

These informal games not only sharpened his skills but also created a sense of belonging and community. Cristiano learned the value of teamwork, an important lesson that would guide him throughout his life. He realized that while individual talent was crucial, true success came from the unity of the team. This understanding of collaboration would echo in his career, reminding him that soccer was about working together as much as it was about individual brilliance.

As the sun set, painting the sky with hues of pink and orange, Cristiano would often stay on the field, practicing his shots alone. These quiet moments were sacred for him—a time to think about his hopes and dreams, imagining a future that felt almost like a fairy tale. The world beyond his little village seemed far away, yet during those precious hours, he nurtured the belief that one day, he would break free from his surroundings.

Cristiano's childhood was a unique mix of innocence and ambition. While most kids his age dreamed of becoming astronauts or superheroes, he dared to picture himself playing on the biggest soccer stages. The thrill of running onto a field filled with fans, the rush of scoring a goal, and the cheers ringing in his ears were visions that fueled his relentless pursuit. His ambition was sparked by the joy of the game, with each kick bringing him closer to making his dreams come true.

In tough times, he found comfort in the biographies of his favorite players, absorbing their stories like treasured lessons. He studied their techniques, their paths, and their struggles, identifying with their relentless drive. These players became his heroes, representing the success he longed for. Little did he know, he was on a journey that would one day make him a source of inspiration for countless others.

As his talent began to shine, local coaches started to notice him. Each recommendation and nod of approval became a stepping stone, nudging him closer to his dreams. The excitement of possibility filled the air like a strong wind, pushing him to chase bigger opportunities beyond the familiar streets of Madeira. Embracing this newfound attention came with a sense of responsibility. He realized that raw talent wasn't enough; he needed to pair it with unwavering dedication and a willingness to go beyond his limits.

Recognizing his growing talent, Cristiano's family made sacrifices to support him. They understood that the road to success is rarely smooth, so they stood by him with unconditional love. Late-night training sessions, weekend tournaments, and the constant hustle to get him into the best teams became their shared reality. In these moments, family bonds grew stronger, and the values of hard work and perseverance became woven into their lives.

The journey from the quiet streets of Madeira to the busy soccer fields of Lisbon was full of uncertainties, yet Cristiano's early experiences formed the grit that would carry him through. Every kick, every training session, and every dream-filled moment brought him closer to his destiny. His path was not without obstacles, but it also sparkled with hope and the promise of something extraordinary.

The essence of his beginnings isn't just a backdrop to his later success; it is the foundation of his entire career. Cristiano Ronaldo, the boy who played soccer with a homemade ball, was meant to rise—not just as an athlete, but as a global icon, inspiring future generations to chase their dreams with relentless passion and determination. His story reminds us all that greatness often comes from the most unassuming beginnings and that with time, effort, and a strong spirit, dreams can grow into something truly remarkable.

Facing Challenges Alone

The moment had arrived for young Cristiano Ronaldo to say goodbye to the cozy warmth of his family and the familiar cobblestone streets of Madeira. At just twelve years old, he found himself on a plane headed for Lisbon, an adventure that felt more daunting than thrilling. The lively energy of the city was a stark contrast to the comfort of his childhood home, where he had spent countless hours dreaming of becoming a soccer star. Now, he was stepping into a world that was both exciting and frightening.

As the plane took off, Cristiano gazed out the window, watching his home shrink into the distance. The lush hills of Madeira, which had once been the backdrop for his endless soccer games, were disappearing, replaced by clouds and the vast expanse of the sky. With each passing moment, the weight of what he was leaving behind settled heavily on his young shoulders. His family—his mother, father, and siblings—were his rock, and the thought of facing the unknown without them filled him with a deep sense of loneliness.

Once he arrived in Lisbon, he was enveloped by the noisy hustle and bustle of the city. People hurried past him, their faces becoming a blur, while the towering buildings loomed overhead like giants. Here, he was just another face in the crowd, a small fish in a vast ocean. The thrill of being at the prestigious Sporting Lisbon Academy was quickly overshadowed by the reality of being away from home, missing home-cooked meals and the comfort of his small bedroom where dreams of stardom felt so tangible.

At the academy, he encountered a whole new set of challenges. The training sessions were tough, demanding both physical strength and mental toughness that Cristiano was still learning to develop. The coaches, while supportive, had high expectations. Driven by his ambition, Cristiano threw himself into the grueling routines, pushing through exhaustion and pain. But after every intense practice, he often found himself alone with his thoughts. While the other boys chatted and laughed, he struggled to connect with the new faces around him.

A flood of emotions washed over him— homesickness crashed over him like a wave, washing away his spirit. The other boys had each other to rely on, forming bonds over shared experiences and common goals. Meanwhile, Cristiano felt like an outsider, a boy from a small island dealing with feelings of not being good enough. After training sessions, he would sneak away to quiet corners of the academy, letting tears slide down his cheeks in moments of vulnerability.

But amidst this emotional storm, a fire burned within him that refused to go out. Determination became his closest ally. Cristiano hadn't left Madeira just to chase a dream; he had set out to embrace the challenges that came with it. He made up his mind that if he wanted to succeed, he would need to outwork everyone else. So, he started waking up before dawn, lacing up his cleats while the city was still wrapped in darkness. The cool morning air welcomed him as he stepped onto the training field, practicing alone—dribbling, shooting, and honing his skills until the sun began to rise.

These early morning routines became his refuge. In those peaceful moments, he found clarity and strength. As the sun painted the sky in bright oranges and pinks, Cristiano envisioned his goals. Every drop of sweat that fell to the ground was a testament to his commitment to his craft. The loneliness that shadowed him during the day faded in the quiet solitude of the mornings, replaced by an unwavering focus on getting better.

Even with all the training and hard work, the challenges didn't let up. The pressure to succeed hung over him like a dark cloud. He watched the other boys, with their easy camaraderie and confident laughter, seemingly breezing through their days. Every goal they scored and every achievement they celebrated reminded him of his struggle to fit in. But instead of letting those feelings derail him, he turned them into motivation.

Cristiano began to carve out his own path through sheer will and relentless dedication. The drills he pushed himself through were demanding, often continuing long after official training ended. While others headed home to relax, he stayed behind to run extra laps or practice shooting from tough angles. In his mind, every drop of blood, sweat, and tears would be worth it in the end. He embraced the discomfort of pushing his limits, knowing that every bit of effort would bring him closer to his dream.

Gradually, the other boys began to notice him. They could see the young player who stayed late on the field, whose determination made him stand out. Slowly but surely, barriers started to break down. Cristiano began forming connections, chipping away at the loneliness with shared drills and friendly competitions. The initial shyness he felt started to fade as he laughed at their jokes, cheered for their victories, and learned to lean on them in moments of self-doubt.

As friendships blossomed, the challenges of being away from home became a little easier. The boys became like brothers, sharing in both the triumphs and the struggles that came with being young athletes. Cristiano realized how important companionship was in overcoming difficulties, understanding that while his journey was his own, the feelings of fear and uncertainty were something everyone shared.

With this new dynamic, the training sessions transformed into something more than just preparation for the future; they became moments of joy, laughter, and shared dreams. The hard work of soccer turned into a bonding experience. They joked about their less-than-perfect techniques and cheered each other on as they stumbled through drills, creating memories that would last a lifetime.

Still, even as he formed friendships, the journey wasn't without its ups and downs. There were days when loneliness crept back in, lurking like a shadow in his mind. When the pressure to perform became overwhelming, he would think of the warmth of his family's hugs, the aroma of his mother's cooking, and the laughter shared with his siblings. In those moments, he longed for home, a place where he was more than just a budding athlete but a beloved son and brother.

Navigating these emotional waves wasn't easy, but it strengthened his resolve. Each challenge he faced became a stepping stone, a lesson in resilience that shaped him into the athlete he dreamed of being. He came to understand that greatness often arises from tough times, and every moment of discomfort was molding him into a stronger version of himself.

Looking back on his journey, it became clear that while the dreams of fame and fortune danced in his head, it was the determination built through hardship that truly mattered. Facing challenges alone taught him to stand tall, embrace vulnerability, and find strength both in solitude and in the company of others. Cristiano Ronaldo, the boy who left his picturesque village for the busy streets of Lisbon, was beginning to transform into a young man who recognized that growth often springs from the discomfort of the unknown.

As he trained day after day, he realized that confronting fears head-on wasn't just a necessary part of the journey but an empowering choice that would shape the rest of his life. The road ahead was long, but each step taken in the early morning light brought him closer to his dreams. With sweat pouring down, he solidified the belief that nothing could hold him back—not loneliness, fear, or the weight of expectations.

In the heart of Lisbon, the boy from Madeira was starting to forge his own identity—one defined not by doubts but by the brilliance of his determination. As the sun set over the city, casting a hopeful glow across the sky, Cristiano knew that the best was yet to come, and he was ready to face whatever challenges lay ahead. The struggles would not define him; they would be the very things that helped him rise, propelling him toward greatness and igniting a passion that would eventually light up the world stage.

Cristiano's journey during those formative years serves as a powerful reminder for anyone facing challenges in their lives. While the road may be filled with obstacles, it's the persistence to push through that leads to personal growth and success. We all encounter moments that test our determination; it's how we respond to those moments that truly shapes who we are.

The Making of a Legend

In the heart of Lisbon, something incredible was about to happen. Imagine a skinny kid, just starting his teenage years, with a messy head of hair and a determination that far exceeded his size. This was Cristiano Ronaldo—an awkward boy with dreams so big they couldn't be contained. Inside him burned a fierce desire to prove himself and change his life. This wasn't just a young athlete finding his way; it was the start of a legend.

As dawn broke over the city, while most of Lisbon was still sound asleep, Cristiano was already on the field, his cleats digging into the damp grass. The cool morning air felt refreshing, but it couldn't compare to the fire inside him. He knew that success wouldn't come to him; he had to chase it down with all his might. So, he trained—day after day—his heart racing in time with the dreams he held tight.

These early mornings became sacred to him, a peaceful time when the world was still, and he could concentrate solely on his craft. As he dribbled, shot, and worked on his footwork, every bead of sweat was proof of his dedication. The sounds of his breath and the city waking up faded into the background. All that mattered was the moment—this was his safe haven, where he could become the athlete he longed to be.

The demanding training sessions at the academy were meant to push the boys to their limits, and Cristiano took that challenge head-on. He wasn't just there to participate; he was there to compete against himself. While others looked for ways to take it easy or catch a break, Cristiano was relentless. The drills that left his teammates panting for air felt like warm-ups to him. These were the moments he cherished, where he could showcase his determination and commitment.

His coaches noticed him. One training session stands out in his memory—a hot day when fatigue threatened to drag everyone down. The boys were running laps around the field for conditioning, and many started to fall behind, some even clutching their sides in exhaustion. But Cristiano? He pushed through the tiredness, his legs feeling heavy, his lungs burning. With every lap, he whispered to himself, "You are strong. You are capable. You are destined for greatness."

When he finished another lap, he could hear his coach's voice cutting through the haze. "Look at Ronaldo! If you want to see what hard work looks like, just watch him!" That moment changed everything for him. His coach's words sparked something inside, igniting a belief that would only grow as his journey unfolded. Praise from authority figures can be a strong motivator, and for Cristiano, it meant more than just compliments; it confirmed he was heading in the right direction.

As days turned into weeks, the loneliness that had once surrounded him began to fade. With newfound confidence came friendship, formed in the heat of competition and respect. The other boys recognized his tenacity and started to rally around him. Together, they built bonds strengthened by their shared love for soccer and their relentless drive to improve. They cheered each other on during victories and lifted each other during defeats. In those moments of togetherness, Cristiano felt a warmth like family—a support system that helped him navigate the ups and downs of his new life.

But not every moment was filled with joy and achievement. There were days when self-doubt crept in unexpectedly. One day, after a tough training session, Cristiano overheard two teammates whispering about a recent tournament where he hadn't played his best. Their words hung in the air, cutting through the warm camaraderie like a cold knife. They talked about his weaknesses, suggesting he didn't belong in the same conversations as the game's stars. For a brief moment, he felt like that skinny kid again—lost, unsure, and adrift.

However, rather than retreat into doubt, he used that hurt as fuel. The next morning, as the city was wrapped in the early light of dawn, Cristiano found himself back on the field, determined to prove them wrong. He pushed himself harder, stayed longer, and set even more ambitious goals. Every practice became a building block, every setback a lesson. He concentrated on his weaknesses, turning them into strengths. In his mind, there was no room for failure; only chances to learn and grow.

A profound realization struck Cristiano: the simple act of working hard was a privilege, a golden opportunity to sharpen his skills and chase his dreams. He began to embrace the sacrifices that came with this path. Birthdays, social events, and fun times with friends faded into the background as he devoted himself to training. It wasn't that he didn't appreciate those moments; he just understood that achieving greatness often requires tough choices.

Making sacrifices also meant saying no to parties where laughter and joy filled the air. He remembered one time when some friends from the academy were planning a weekend gathering, the kind where laughter echoed and friendships deepened. The atmosphere was electric, and part of him wanted to join in, to feel that connection outside of the training field. But deep down, he realized that while they were celebrating, he would be honing his game, refining his skills. And so, he chose the field.

This unwavering commitment eventually led him to a pivotal moment in his budding career—a local tournament that showcased the most promising talents from the region. For Cristiano, this was a chance to prove himself not just to his friends but to the larger soccer community. As the tournament drew near, he poured all his energy into preparing, visualizing success and pushing himself to be his best.

On the day of the tournament, excitement and nerves coursed through him like electricity. His heart raced as he stepped onto the pitch, the stands filled with spectators eager to see the talent on display. Under the bright lights, he felt both exhilarated and anxious. The pressure was intense; this was the moment he had been training for.

As the match kicked off, Cristiano found his groove, weaving between defenders and making plays with skill. He felt unstoppable, as if he were soaring, a whirlwind of passion and talent. Then, in a split second that felt like forever, the ball landed at his feet just outside the penalty box. With precise control, he turned and sent a powerful strike curling beautifully into the top corner of the net. The crowd erupted into cheers, a sound that washed over him, lifting him higher than he had ever imagined.

That goal was a significant milestone in his journey. Not only did it secure victory for his team, but it also brought him the recognition he had been working so hard for. Scouts began to notice him, and whispers of his talent circulated through the soccer community. For the boy from Madeira, this was a breakthrough—a taste of the glory he had fervently pursued.

The thrill of that moment stayed with him, echoing in his heart and fueling his desire for even more accomplishments. Yet, he knew this was just the beginning. Each achievement only deepened his hunger for more. Recognition became a stepping stone, not a final destination. With every goal scored and every compliment received, he understood that the true essence of his journey lay not in accolades but in the tireless pursuit of excellence.

Cristiano Ronaldo's transformation from a skinny kid to a powerful athlete was about more than just physical training; it was about nurturing a mindset rooted in hard work, sacrifice, and an unwavering belief in himself. His journey was marked by countless hours spent perfecting his skills, enduring pain, and pushing beyond limits that might have stopped others.

As he climbed the ranks, he learned that the path to greatness is a long-distance race, not a sprint. The sweat, the tears, the loneliness—they all played a role in shaping his destiny. In his heart, he knew that with every challenge faced and every sacrifice made, he was building the groundwork for something extraordinary. The boy who once stood alone on the practice field was now a force to be reckoned with—a shining example of hard work and resilience.

Ronaldo's story invites each of us to think about our own dreams. What aspirations are waiting to be pursued? What sacrifices are we willing to make? Though every path has its obstacles, it's the readiness to show up, to work hard, and to believe in ourselves that truly makes the difference. Ronaldo's journey reminds us that while talent can give us a start, it is hard work and dedication that lead to real success.

In those quiet moments when self-doubt sneaks in and the comfort of ease calls, it's the spirit of persistence that sets legends apart from the crowd. Cristiano Ronaldo's story encourages each of us to embrace our dreams, work diligently towards them, and realize that greatness is not just a destination; it's a lifelong journey filled with hard work, resilience, and passion. Whether in sports, school, or any personal goal, the same principles apply: with perseverance and effort, anything is possible.

Chapter 2: The Little Magician: Lionel Messi's Magical Journey

Defying the Odds

Lionel Messi's story starts not on a grand soccer field filled with cheering fans, but in the simple surroundings of Rosario, Argentina. It was here that he took his first steps into a world that would one day celebrate his incredible talent. Born into a family that loved soccer, Messi was surrounded by the sport from a young age, often watching his father, who worked in a steel factory and coached, share his passion for the game. As a child, Messi was just a regular boy, smaller than many, but his love for soccer was undeniable. Little did he know, his early journey would be filled with challenges that would test his strength and spirit.

At just 11 years old, Messi faced a diagnosis that would frighten many parents: growth hormone deficiency. This condition meant that his body didn't produce enough hormones for normal growth. Imagine being a young boy dreaming of becoming a professional soccer player, but realizing that your body isn't keeping up with those dreams. It would be easy for many to give up in such a situation, but not Messi. Instead of letting despair take over, he turned the news into a reason to fight back.

Every day, Messi had to go through painful hormone injections, a routine that would make most kids cringe. But he stayed determined, showing a maturity beyond his years. While other kids were caught up in school, video games, and the usual fun of youth, Messi woke up with a singular focus on his dreams—both on and off the field. Deep down, he believed that he could make his dreams come true and become the player he so desperately wanted to be.

What's truly inspiring about Messi's story is how he turned this obstacle into motivation. While others might have seen impossible odds, Messi found inspiration in them. Every training session became a chance to build resilience. While some young athletes may have been discouraged by being different, Messi embraced it. He transformed what others saw as weaknesses into strengths. Sure, he was smaller than his peers, but he compensated with remarkable speed, agility, and a unique understanding of the game. His low center of gravity allowed him to maneuver around defenders with a grace that left many in awe.

As he kept developing his skills on the soccer field, Messi's hard work began to pay off. The local club, Newell's Old Boys, recognized his extraordinary talent and invited him to join their youth team. This was a place where he could improve alongside peers who shared his love for the sport. However, the journey wasn't easy. The cost of Messi's hormone treatments put a significant strain on his family. His father's modest income as a factory worker couldn't cover the growing expenses, and the pressure was evident. But instead of giving in to hardship, the Messi family showed unity and determination. They believed wholeheartedly in Lionel's potential, providing constant support and encouragement.

Messi's story is also about the importance of teamwork. As he continued to grow as a player, he learned how crucial it was to work with others. The friendships he formed with his teammates became vital as they experienced victories and losses together, learning valuable life lessons on and off the field. Messi discovered that while he had exceptional skills, true success often comes from a group of people working together toward a shared goal.

The challenges Messi faced helped him build a strong mindset. As he moved up the ranks at Newell's, he approached each game with an unquenchable hunger. Each dribble, goal, and assist fueled his passion. He became more than just a player; he was a force to be reckoned with. The pitch became his safe haven, a place where he could express himself and transform his struggles into something beautiful. He wasn't just playing soccer; he was turning dreams into reality.

But this was only the beginning of his incredible journey. As Messi's talent became clearer, scouts from around the world started to take notice. At just 13, he faced a life-changing choice: stay in Argentina, where he felt at home, or chase his dreams in Europe. Leaving behind his family and everything familiar was intimidating. Many young athletes would find such a decision overwhelming. Yet, for Messi, the chance for greatness outweighed his fears. With a heavy heart, he made the brave choice to board a plane to Spain, where FC Barcelona was ready to welcome him.

This move came with its own set of challenges. Arriving in a new country, Messi had to adjust to a culture very different from his own. He was just a young boy in a foreign land, trying to learn a new language and navigate a different lifestyle. But once again, he showed resilience. While many would have felt lost, he saw an opportunity to grow, learn, and build his own legacy. Through hard work, he found a supportive community at Barcelona, where coaches and teammates recognized his raw talent and helped him develop it.

Messi's time at Barcelona would become legendary, but it wasn't without obstacles. Adapting to life in a prestigious academy pushed him even harder. The competition was tough, with many other talented young players vying for the spotlight. It was there that Messi learned the value of humility and hard work. He realized that natural talent alone wouldn't cut it; dedication was just as important. While others might have relied on their gifts, Messi combined his natural abilities with a fierce work ethic that made him stand out. He practiced tirelessly, spending hours refining his skills, learning from mistakes, and perfecting his techniques. He wasn't just a player; he was a dedicated student of the game.

As Messi blossomed, he started to gain attention not just from coaches, but from the entire soccer world. His name echoed through the halls of Camp Nou, and fans were amazed by his ability to glide through defenders like they were mere shadows. But for Messi, it was never about fame; it was about his love for the game. Each time he stepped onto the field, he felt a thrill that came from doing what he loved most. This genuine passion made him beloved by fans and earned him respect from fellow players.

As time went on, Messi became a symbol of hope and a reminder that perseverance can help one overcome life's challenges. His story isn't just about talent; it's a tale of resilience, showing us that obstacles can be turned into stepping stones. Messi's journey stands as an enduring light for aspiring athletes and dreamers everywhere, proving that the road to greatness is often filled with hurdles that require bravery and determination.

Even as he broke records and collected trophies, Messi never forgot the struggles of his early years. He stayed humble, recognizing that his success was not just due to his hard work, but also the support of those who believed in him. Every trophy he lifted paid tribute to the lessons he learned along the way—the importance of hard work, the value of community, and the strength of resilience. His journey from the streets of Rosario to the grand stadiums of Europe resonates deeply, reflecting the experiences of countless young athletes who dare to dream.

By facing his challenges and turning them into strengths, Messi embodies the true spirit of perseverance. He reminds us that, no matter how tough things may seem, the odds can be overcome. His journey encourages every aspiring player dealing with their own struggles to find their voice and keep pushing forward despite the difficulties. Messi's story teaches us that it's not the obstacles we encounter that shape us, but how we respond to them that defines our character and ultimately our future.

Mastering the Ball

While many kids are lucky enough to kick around shiny, brand-new soccer balls, Lionel Messi's beginnings were quite different.

Young Messi had to think outside the box and use whatever he could find to sharpen his skills. One of his most beloved training tools was, surprisingly, an orange. Yes, you heard that right—an orange! Picture this: a little boy weaving around his house, carefully dribbling the round fruit with his small feet, all while dreaming of a stadium filled with cheering fans and bright lights shining down on him.

In this image, we see the heart of Messi's approach to soccer. He practiced with endless determination, dodging imaginary defenders in his living room and pouring every ounce of youthful energy into perfecting his footwork. Excuses and limitations simply didn't exist in Messi's world—just a single-minded focus on becoming the best. That humble orange became a symbol of his creativity, grit, and a reminder that real skill often grows from the simplest beginnings.

Messi's story with his orange is a powerful reminder of how innovation and resourcefulness can lead to greatness. While many young athletes might think they need the latest gear or perfect fields to succeed, Messi took the ordinary and made it extraordinary. He embraced what life offered him, and instead of complaining about his situation, he found joy in creating opportunities. He turned something as simple as an orange into a training partner, all while relishing the process.

The world witnessed how he transformed those childhood makeshift tools into a lifelong journey of mastering the beautiful game.

As he practiced day after day, Messi started to build a special bond with the ball. His dedication was clear; he knew that to reach the top of the soccer world, he had to go beyond what everyone else expected. The dribbles, the flicks, and the turns became smoother and more graceful, as he formed a connection with the ball that few could ever match. It was as if the very spirit of the game flowed through him, making him an artist and the ball his canvas.

But it wasn't just Messi's determination that made this story special; it was also a profound lesson about how creativity can open doors, even when resources are limited. In a world that often ties success to money or fancy facilities, Messi's journey shows us that sometimes all it takes is a bit of imagination and an unwavering work ethic. His orange was not just a training tool; it became a metaphor for the joy of making the best out of any situation.

Imagine this: a young Messi, dribbling around his house, skillfully navigating through imaginary defenders as he learns various tricks and techniques. He embraced the challenge of using something as simple as an orange to practice, knowing that every hour spent perfecting his craft would bring him closer to his dream. The essence of Messi's spirit shines through in those moments of dedication. His determination turned the everyday into something magical as he poured his heart and soul into the simple act of mastering the ball.

As Messi's skills blossomed, he realized that mastery isn't just about talent. It's also about persistence, creativity, and finding joy in the game. The best in any field aren't just those born with talent; they're the ones who keep pushing, exploring, and practicing. They take the ordinary and elevate it into something extraordinary. Messi understood this deeply, which is why he was ready to embrace the playful challenge of dribbling an orange in his quest for greatness.

There's something incredibly inspiring about picturing a young boy practicing with an orange. It vividly shows the power of perseverance and the importance of enjoying the journey to greatness. While many might have only seen a piece of fruit, Messi saw a chance to shape his future. His experience invites us to think: what barriers are we creating for ourselves? What resources do we have around us that we might be overlooking?

Next time you find yourself struggling with your own passions—be it sports, art, or any pursuit—remember Messi and his orange. It's a reminder that creativity can spark progress, and that joy in the process is a lesson worth learning. There are no perfect conditions or ideal situations—just the willingness to embrace what you have and make the most of it.

Messi's journey was not just about dribbling; it was a continuous path of growth and self-discovery. As he polished his skills, he began to grasp the intricacies of the game—the strategic positioning, timing, and the unspoken connections between players on the field. He learned to read defenders' movements and anticipate their next steps. The orange, in its own special way, helped him develop a sense of space, balance, and control.

His early experiences taught him that success doesn't come overnight. Instead, it's the result of countless hours spent practicing, stumbling, and getting back up again. Messi's readiness to face challenges head-on and to look beyond the surface of obstacles laid the groundwork for his future successes. Each day spent with his makeshift training tool was a stepping stone on his soccer journey.

Even as he climbed the ranks of youth soccer and eventually joined FC Barcelona, the lessons he learned during those formative years stuck with him. The creativity he harnessed while mastering the ball became a defining trait of his playing style. He continued to discover innovative ways to navigate the pitch, even when facing the toughest opponents.

As we watch Messi dazzle on the field, it's easy to forget the roots of his talent. The extraordinary dribbles, the stunning goals, and the effortless grace are all the results of years spent perfecting his craft with whatever he had. His success wasn't just about raw talent; it was the outcome of relentless practice, creativity, and a deep passion for the game.

So, as you reflect on your own dreams and goals, think about the lessons from Messi's journey with his orange. What does mastery look like for you? How can you approach your passions with a sense of creativity and playfulness? Each of us has the ability to find unique solutions to our challenges, just like Messi did that day with his orange.

Messi's story resonates with anyone who has ever pursued a passion. It reminds us that it's not always the resources we have that dictate our success, but our mindset and the choices we make. Mastery is about exploring, experimenting, and finding joy in the journey. The next time you feel tempted to dismiss your potential due to circumstances, remember Lionel Messi and his simple yet profound approach to mastering the ball. After all, the most remarkable achievements often start with the tiniest of ideas and the most unexpected of inspirations.

A Star Is Born

The roar of the crowd surged like a wave crashing against the shore, and you could feel the energy buzzing in the air. This was a moment that would forever be etched in the history of soccer—the very first time Lionel Messi scored for FC Barcelona's youth team. Picture it: a sun-soaked field, the scent of freshly cut grass mixed with the excitement of young athletes all around. Every heartbeat matched the thrill in the stands, and in that charged atmosphere, a young boy was about to etch his name into the story of the beautiful game.

When Messi received the ball, it felt like time slowed down, creating a scene you'd expect in a movie, where every detail pops. His small frame held an extraordinary talent, and with that first touch, it was clear—this wasn't just any player. He zipped past defenders with a fluidity that made it seem like he was floating, a whirlwind of determination and skill. The ball danced at his feet, as if it were an extension of him. The spectators couldn't believe their eyes, their faces lit up with awe. This was pure magic happening right on the pitch.

As he sped forward, Messi's thoughts raced. Would he miss? Would the defenders catch up to him? Doubts always linger around dreams, but he had prepared for this moment—day after day, practicing until his legs

felt heavy and his feet ached. There was no
space for fear; just an intense desire to make
his dreams come true. He wasn't just playing;
he was proving that all his hard work was
leading to something big.

When the ball hit the back of the net, it
sent shockwaves through the crowd. The
eruption of cheers was overwhelming, a loud
mix of excitement that rang in Messi's ears. He
turned to his teammates, arms raised high in
victory, a smile spreading across his face that
seemed to glow with pure joy. It was more than
just a goal; it was a statement. The little boy
who once faced countless hurdles had made
his mark. No longer just a dreamer, he was
now a young soccer star on the brink of
something great.

That moment captured the essence of
hard work, determination, and self-belief. It
wasn't just about the thrill of scoring; it was a
tribute to all the sacrifices he made—long nights
practicing in the family yard, early mornings
perfecting his skills, and the steadfast support
of his family. Each of these elements played a
part in this defining moment. Messi
understood that while the crowd cheered,
every cheer echoed the struggles he had faced.

Messi's journey wasn't just a tale of a
boy with talent; it became a source of
inspiration for anyone chasing a dream. It
reminded us all that the greatest achievements

in life often come from persistence and resilience. The road to success is rarely straight; it's filled with bumps and detours. Every setback, every moment of doubt, was just a stepping stone leading him to that euphoric goal—the moment that changed everything.

As he celebrated with his teammates, the world outside that field faded into the background. It was just Messi, the ball, and the electrifying feeling of having made it—though it was only the beginning of his incredible journey. In that joyous celebration, he embodied the essence of believing in oneself. The roar of the crowd became the soundtrack to his dreams, pushing him to move forward. More challenges would come, but this moment reminded him of why he started in the first place.

The lessons from that day extend far beyond the soccer field. They touch the heart of the human experience: take hold of every opportunity that life throws your way. Each chance to showcase your talent is a potential milestone, a stepping stone toward something greater. Just like Messi, when the spotlight shines bright, be ready to embrace it with open arms. What you achieve in those moments can leave a lasting impact, inspiring others who are on their own paths.

For every young dreamer out there, Messi's first goal stands as proof that greatness isn't solely about raw talent. It's about preparation, persistence, and an unyielding spirit. Remember, there will be days when the journey feels tough and the odds seem impossible. On those days, let Messi's story remind you that every challenge is an opportunity waiting to be seized. Every obstacle you face can turn into motivation if you allow it.

As Messi went on to score countless more goals, the magic of that first strike never faded from his heart. Each new achievement was driven by the unwavering belief that he truly belonged on that stage, competing with the best. That goal was a spark, igniting a fire that would blaze through his career, lighting his way through success, fame, and the admiration of millions.

In many ways, Messi's story teaches us about the mixed nature of dreams—they can be both thrilling and intimidating. They carry expectations and the fear of failure. Yet, when we face those fears with open hearts and willing spirits, amazing things can happen. The scoreboard may count points, but the true measure of success lies in the growth we experience along the way.

So, what can we learn from this incredible moment in Messi's early career? It's straightforward: never underestimate the power of believing in yourself. Recognize the hurdles you face and take pride in your journey, no matter how tough it seems. Life will present challenges, but with determination and a fierce spirit, your moment will come too. Like Messi, you may find yourself standing in the spotlight, arms raised in triumph, celebrating not just a goal, but the extraordinary journey that got you there.

The importance of that first goal echoes beyond the pitch. It's a story for anyone chasing their passions, reminding us all that we have the ability to turn dreams into reality. So, welcome every opportunity with open arms and ready feet. You never know when your defining moment will arrive, but when it does, make sure you're prepared to shine. The world is waiting, and greatness is just within your grasp.

Chapter 3: Golden Goals: Alex Morgan's Path to Glory

A Setback Becomes a Comeback

It was a sunny Friday afternoon, the kind of day that made the grass look extra vibrant, as Alex Morgan laced up her cleats, feeling a mix of excitement and nervous energy. She had become a familiar face on her high school soccer team, a symbol of hope and skill for her teammates and coaches alike. When the whistle blew, signaling the start of the game, the cheers from her classmates filled the air, urging her on. But in the blink of an eye, that hopeful energy shifted into something far more serious—a sharp snap echoed through the field, and everything changed.

Suddenly, the world around her felt like it was moving in slow motion. Time seemed to freeze as an intense pain shot through her leg, a sensation like nothing she had ever known. The bright sun felt dimmed, and the joyful cheers of her friends faded into a haunting silence. It hit her like a ton of bricks: this was more than just a bruise or a sprain; it was a serious injury that could put her dreams on hold. Lying there on the grass, tears streamed down her face—not just because of the pain but from the fear of what this meant for her future. What would happen to her soccer career? Could she still chase after her dreams?

As she was carried off the field, Alex could see the worry on the faces of her friends and family, their excitement replaced with concern. Each worried glance was a reminder of the uncertainty looming over her. Would she ever play soccer again? Was this the end of her time on the field? This emotional rollercoaster was something few people, especially young athletes, truly understand unless they've lived it. Fear twisted in her stomach as she replayed the moment over and over, questioning everything.

Yet, amidst the storm of emotions, something started to shift inside her. It wasn't an instant change, but rather a small spark of resilience that began to glow. It's like that little flicker of hope that appears when you need it the most, lighting your path in dark times. Alex began to remember all the hard work that had brought her to this moment—every early morning practice, every late-night training session, and every dream she had of becoming a professional athlete. She realized that this setback could actually be a setup for a comeback.

Recovery became her new challenge, and she faced it with the same drive she showed on the soccer field. While some might have sunk into self-pity, Alex chose a different path. With her family's support and her unyielding determination, she created an innovative rehabilitation plan. Swimming became her sanctuary, where the buoyancy of the water allowed her to stay active without straining her injured leg. Each stroke in the pool reminded her that she could still move forward, even if it wasn't on solid ground. She wasn't just healing; she was pushing her own limits.

In addition to swimming, Alex engaged in specialized training to keep her fitness levels up. This was no easy task. It took countless hours of hard work and a lot of courage to face her fears. Doubts crept in like unwanted guests, whispering worries about whether she'd ever regain her speed, agility, or power on the field. But every time those questions arose, she turned them into fuel for her fire.

Every workout became a personal challenge, and each day was another chance to grow. As she fought through the pain and mental obstacles, Alex discovered a strength within herself she hadn't realized was there. She was not just coming back from an injury; she was transforming into a more determined version of herself. Patience became her ally, and she learned that recovery isn't a race—it's a journey.

Then, after what felt like forever, the day arrived when she stood in front of her doctor, her heart racing with anticipation. This moment was more than just about being physically ready; it was the result of all the hard work, sweat, and tears she had invested in her recovery. When he finally gave her the green light to return to the field, joy flooded her heart like a burst dam, releasing all the hopes and dreams that had felt so distant during her rehab.

Returning to the field, with the sun shining brightly above her, felt like coming home. Every sprint, every pass, and every shot on goal became a celebration of her resilience and determination. Overcoming her injury not only changed her approach to soccer but also reshaped how she viewed life. The lessons she learned during those challenging months would serve as the foundation for her character and future achievements.

Deep down, Alex knew that setbacks could turn into stepping stones. She felt a strong desire to share this lesson with others, especially young athletes facing their own hurdles. We all encounter challenges, and it's how we respond to those moments that truly defines us. When we see obstacles as chances to grow, we spark a fire within that pushes us closer to our dreams. Alex's story serves as a reminder that even when the path gets rocky, perseverance can lead to incredible victories.

Making History

The atmosphere at the 2012 Olympic Games was absolutely electric. Fans filled the stands, a lively mix of colors and excitement that pulsed with energy. Flags waved, chants rang out, and the buzz of anticipation wrapped around everyone present like a warm embrace. The U.S. Women's National Soccer Team was about to face off against their biggest rivals, Canada, in the semifinals—a match that would become a standout moment in Alex Morgan's career. The stakes couldn't have been higher; the Olympic dream was at risk, and every player felt the weight of that reality.

As the players lined up for the national anthem, the moment felt monumental. Alex stood side by side with her teammates, her heart racing in sync with the stirring notes that filled the stadium. This was it—the result of countless hours of practice, sweat, and unwavering passion. The crowd erupted into cheers that sent shivers down her spine. Taking a deep breath, she anchored herself in the moment, ready to seize the opportunity.

Kickoff marked the start of a heart-pounding battle. The match unfolded with an intensity that felt almost surreal. The players darted across the field like skilled dancers, executing plays with impressive precision. Canada struck first, scoring an early goal that left the American team in shock. Alex watched her teammates rally with fierce determination. This was more than just a game; it was a fight for their Olympic lives.

With every passing minute, the tension grew thicker. Alex could feel it deep in her bones—the pressure to perform, the urgent need to respond. Time slipped away, and soon the Americans found themselves down by a goal, facing the grim possibility of elimination. But one thing Alex had learned during her recovery journey was the power of resilience. She refused to let doubt creep in. Instead, she concentrated on what needed to be done. The game was far from over.

The turning point came when Abby Wambach, a powerhouse and veteran of the team, equalized with a soaring header that struck the crossbar and crashed into the net. The crowd erupted in thunderous applause, sending an electric jolt through Alex. The U.S. team was back in the game, and with that goal came a renewed sense of hope and determination. As they pushed forward, the intensity only grew. Each pass, tackle, and sprint was fueled by the urgency of the moment.

But just when it seemed like the momentum had shifted, Canada struck again, taking the lead with just minutes left on the clock. The disbelief was palpable; you could almost feel the silence settle over the crowd like a thick fog. Alex's heart sank. Yet, just as the game seemed to slip away, the U.S. team rallied once more, determined to claw their way back into the match.

As the seconds ticked down, the players dug deep, summoning every ounce of strength and spirit. The sound of the referee's whistle signaled the closing moments of the match, and the urgency was electric. The U.S. had to find a way, to seize that fleeting chance. It was now or never.

And then, it happened.

With only seconds remaining, the ball found its way to Alex, who had positioned herself just outside the penalty area. Everything around her faded, the crowd's cheers turned into a distant hum, and all she could see was the goal in front of her. In that split second, it felt like time stood still. Taking a deep breath, she unleashed a shot so precise and powerful that it felt like art in motion. The ball soared past the goalkeeper, rippling the net as it hit home—this goal would go down as the latest scored in Olympic history.

The eruption that followed was deafening. A wave of noise crashed over her as the weight of her accomplishment sank in. Teammates rushed to her, their faces glowing with disbelief and joy, lifting her high into the air. It was a moment of pure triumph, an explosion of emotion that left them all breathless. "Did you see that? No one thought she could do it!" one of her teammates shouted, their voice barely audible over the roaring crowd.

In that moment, all the struggles of her recovery—the fears, the doubts—melted away, replaced by a powerful sense of pride and unity. The energy of the team shone through, a testament to the strength of perseverance and teamwork. They weren't just a group of athletes; they were family, connected by shared experiences and a relentless quest for greatness. Every player on that field had contributed to this moment, and together, they had created something remarkable.

When the final whistle blew, sealing their victory, the realization hit Alex like a wave. They were headed to the Olympic final, a shot at the gold medal. The thrill of victory surged through her as she embraced her teammates, tears of joy streaming down their faces—tears of relief and accomplishment. All the hard work and sacrifices had paid off, and together they had made history.

In the days that followed, as they prepared for the final match, Alex reflected on her journey. She thought about her injury and the tough road to recovery that had transformed her into a stronger, more resilient player. That setback had been painful, yes, but it had also sparked a fire within her, igniting a passion that drove her performance on the field.

Winning that semifinal match was more than just a ticket to the next round; it was about living out the lessons she had learned along the way. The significance of teamwork, the strength of self-belief, and the ability to rise after falling were now woven into her very being. They were the threads that made up her character, and she wore them proudly as she stepped onto the field for the final.

As the sun dipped below the horizon, casting a golden light over the stadium, Alex felt ready to face whatever challenges awaited her. The journey to Olympic glory was still unfolding, but with every step, she was getting closer to her dreams. The fire inside her burned brightly, a beacon of hope and determination guiding her through the challenges ahead.

Inspiring a Generation

Hey there, readers! Have you ever thought about being a hero in your own story? Just like Alex Morgan! If there's one thing Alex shows us, it's that everyone can be a shining light of hope and inspiration—not just for themselves, but for so many others, too. She's taken the soccer world by storm, and it's not just about the trophies or the awards; it's about how she inspires a whole generation of young athletes to dream big and work hard to reach those dreams.

Picture this: a little girl, maybe around eight years old, stands in her backyard. She's wearing oversized cleats that make her trip over her own feet. A soccer ball is nestled between her legs, and her ponytail bounces with excitement as she mimics her favorite players. Perhaps she has seen clips of the U.S. Women's National Soccer Team celebrating a big win. Maybe she's watched Alex Morgan score a goal, her infectious smile lighting up the screen. In that moment, she sees a chance to be part of something grander, something beyond just the game.

Alex Morgan is not just a player; she's become a symbol of what happens when you refuse to let challenges get in your way. Let's take a closer look at what makes her such an inspiring figure, especially her amazing achievement of becoming the youngest American to score 100 international goals. This isn't just a number; it shows her determination, hard work, and dedication.

That milestone wasn't just luck; it was the result of years of commitment, endless hours of practice, and a deep belief in herself and her teammates. Think about it: scoring 100 goals for your country? That's incredible! It says a lot about her talent, but even more, it highlights her love for the game and the journey it took to get there. With every goal she scored, she inspired young girls everywhere to put on their cleats and hit the field, showing them that their dreams were well within reach.

What really makes Alex stand out is her passion for lifting others as she climbs. This isn't just about the bright lights of the stadium or the cheers from fans; it's about being a true leader in sports. Alex knows her influence is far-reaching, and she's made it her mission to ensure that young athletes, especially girls, have the chances and support they need to succeed. It's like she carries a torch, lighting the way for those who will follow in her footsteps, guiding them through paths that might have once felt dark and uncertain.

Through various programs, Alex focuses on empowering young female athletes to believe in themselves and their skills. She supports initiatives that encourage girls to play soccer, highlighting the importance of teamwork and resilience. Imagine her speaking to a group of eager players, her enthusiasm infectious as she shares her own story, the challenges she faced, and how she overcame them. Her message hits home: "Don't let anything hold you back! Your dreams matter, and you can achieve great things!"

In her quest to inspire, Alex takes on the role of a mentor, showing that being a top player also means being a role model. Her approach to sports and life is about community. She understands the weight of her influence and embraces it with open arms, engaging with young athletes in ways that truly matter. Her presence at youth camps and clinics, her advocacy for equal opportunities in sports, and her honesty about her own struggles make her relatable and admired. She isn't just an athlete; she's a friend, a guide, and a source of encouragement.

Take a moment to think about your own life. Has someone ever inspired you? Maybe it was a coach who saw your potential when you couldn't see it yourself, or a teacher who believed in you even when you had doubts. Alex embodies that spirit, reminding us that we all can lift each other up. And what's beautiful is that her influence goes beyond the soccer field. Young athletes are not just motivated to score goals; they're encouraged to be kind, to work hard, and to stand up for what they believe in.

As we celebrate Alex's achievements, we also need to recognize the responsibility that comes with being a leader. With great power comes great responsibility, and Alex understands this deeply. Her platform allows her to speak out on issues that resonate with young athletes, like gender equality in sports, body positivity, and mental health awareness. In a world where girls are often told to play small, she pushes them to be bold, to chase their passions fiercely, and to challenge the limits that society tries to impose.

Imagine the conversations that unfold as young girls come together to play soccer, inspired by Alex's story. They talk about teamwork, friendship, and the joy of the game. They share dreams of scoring the winning goal, playing in front of cheering crowds, and making a difference in their communities. They see Alex as a reflection of their own dreams, reminding them that they, too, can rewrite their stories and break through barriers.

This beautiful cycle of inspiration is what makes Alex Morgan an extraordinary figure in sports. She doesn't just play to win; she plays to empower. She doesn't just score goals; she opens doors. Her journey tells us a lot about the power of resilience, the strength of a supportive community, and the importance of lifting others as you rise.

As we think about the impact of Alex's story, let's also consider our own roles in shaping the next generation. How can we be a light for those around us? How can we create a space that nurtures growth, encourages dreams, and supports perseverance? Maybe it's through mentoring, whether formally or informally, or just being there for someone who needs a little boost. It might involve sharing your own challenges and successes, showing others that setbacks are just steps on the road to success.

In a world that often seems full of obstacles, stories like Alex Morgan's remind us that we can conquer adversity with hard work and determination. As you finish this chapter, take a moment to reflect on your own dreams. What are the goals that spark your passion? What steps can you take today to get closer to them?

Next time you kick a soccer ball or grab your favorite sports gear, think of Alex Morgan. Think about her journey, her strength, and her commitment to lifting those around her. You might find that the heart of sports is not just competition but also the connections we create, the lives we touch, and the inspiration we share. Remember, your story is just as important as hers, and you have the power to make a positive difference, one goal at a time.

So, what will your legacy be? Dream big, work hard, and remember: every goal, every challenge, and every victory is a piece of your unique journey. The world is waiting for your story—let's make it one that inspires others to chase their dreams with the same passion that Alex has shown throughout her amazing career. Together, let's turn those dreams into reality.

W. Bo Cricklewood

Chapter 4: King of the Game: Just Call Him Pelé

From Grapefruits to Glory

Imagine a young boy named Edson Arantes do Nascimento, but most people know him as Pelé. Picture him racing barefoot through the sunlit streets of Bauru, Brazil. The air is filled with the smell of fresh fruit and the friendly chatter of neighbors. But all of that fades as he weaves between trees and jumps over rocks, his heart bursting with joy. In his hands, he grips a grapefruit—his very own soccer ball. While other kids might have been kicking around shiny, new soccer balls, Pelé cleverly turned his surroundings into a playground, pouring his passion into something truly special.

In this small town, life was tough for Pelé's family, who often struggled to make ends meet. His dad, a professional soccer player, had been injured, and his mom took on the heavy load of supporting the family. Even though times were hard, they raised Pelé to be resilient and resourceful, qualities that would shape his future. Every day, as he skillfully juggled the grapefruit—his pride and joy—he was not just practicing soccer; he was building a mindset that would help him overcome whatever came his way.

Imagine Pelé in those lively days of his youth, sprinting down the cracked sidewalks. With every bounce of the grapefruit, he pictured himself playing alongside Brazil's soccer legends. His heroes, Zizinho and Bile, inspired him not only with their amazing talent but with their unwavering spirit. He would imitate their moves, creating a world in his mind where he was scoring goals in front of thousands of cheering fans, even though he was just a boy in a humble neighborhood.

What Pelé lacked in fancy equipment, he more than made up for with determination. It was like turning lemons into lemonade—or rather, turning grapefruits into glory. He practiced day and night, using whatever he could find as a goal, from old crates to carefully stacked stones. The laughter of his friends and the occasional teasing only pushed him harder. Deep down, he knew something important: greatness doesn't depend on having the best stuff, but on having a strong spirit and the willingness to put in the effort.

As he raced through the dusty streets, each kick of the grapefruit was a lesson in creativity. Sure, the ball wasn't the right shape or size, but Pelé learned to control it as if it were the most perfect soccer ball ever made. He became skilled at improvising, finding ways to mimic the game's finer points without any formal training or fancy gear. This is something young readers can think about: What challenges are they facing that require a little creativity and a fresh perspective? Pelé's journey serves as a powerful reminder that limitations can become stepping stones on the path to success.

His parents cheered him on, knowing that soccer could offer a glimpse of hope for a better future. While they couldn't buy the latest gear, they provided encouragement in other meaningful ways. Their sacrifices taught him the importance of hard work and commitment. Every evening, as the sun dipped below the horizon and the stars began to twinkle, Pelé chased his dreams. He became known as the boy with the grapefruit, a nickname that reflected both his ambition and his fiery passion.

Kids in the neighborhood gathered to watch him play, their laughter echoing in the air as they cheered for the dreamer among them. Each practice was a performance, showing everyone what was possible when creativity met determination. Pelé's story illustrates how being resourceful can turn tough situations into advantages. Like Edson, many young readers might find themselves facing challenges. The trick is to look beyond those obstacles and see how they can shape your path.

As the grapefruit soared through the air, Pelé often closed his eyes and imagined the cheers of a stadium. He pictured himself, just sixteen years old, stepping onto the grandest stage of all—the World Cup. But before that dream could come true, he had to believe in himself and commit to countless hours of practice. Every time he picked up that grapefruit, it represented not just play but the journey of self-improvement. The message here is clear: dreams need hard work and perseverance, and it's in the daily grind that passion turns into purpose.

And here's a question for all of us, especially for the young dreamers reading this: what are your grapefruits? What obstacles are standing in your way, and how can you turn them into opportunities? This question invites self-reflection, encouraging readers to think about their resources, no matter how modest they may be, and to consider how they can pursue their passions creatively.

Pelé refused to let his circumstances decide his future. Instead, he transformed every challenge into a step toward greatness. The laughter of the children and the cheers from the neighborhood became a soundtrack for his early days, inspiring him to reach for the stars. His ability to see potential where others saw barriers helped him develop a mindset that would benefit him for years to come.

From a young boy navigating the streets of Bauru with a grapefruit to becoming a global soccer icon, Pelé's story stands as a remarkable testament to the power of creativity, resilience, and the unshakable belief in one's dreams. It calls out to every young reader not just to recognize their dreams, but to find the courage to chase them, no matter the hurdles they might encounter.

In those early years, Pelé built the foundation for a legacy that would inspire generations to come. His journey teaches us that even the humblest beginnings can lead to extraordinary achievements if one is willing to work hard, adapt, and dream without limits.

A Teenage Champion

As time went by, Pelé wasn't just that young boy running barefoot through the sunny streets of Bauru, Brazil, with a grapefruit in hand anymore. He was changing—both in his skills and his presence. At just 15 years old, he was on the edge of a life-changing adventure that would take him to greatness. The struggles of his childhood, filled with sacrifice and determination, were just the beginning of an exciting journey ahead.

Soccer was already the heartbeat of Pelé's life. Every single day, he dedicated himself to rigorous training, practicing tirelessly to sharpen his skills. His mornings started before the sun fully came up. He would lace up his worn-out shoes and head to the nearest field, with dew sparkling on the grass. Each practice felt like a promise to himself, a commitment to his dreams that rang loudly in his heart. He had no time for taking it easy; he had a future to chase.

Then came the day that changed everything: his first professional contract with Santos FC. This wasn't just a big moment; it was a turning point that echoed through his life and the history of soccer. As he signed that contract, sealing his fate, Pelé felt a rush of emotions—joy mixed with a bit of nervousness. The weight of expectation hung in the air, but so did the excitement of what was to come.

When he made his debut, the atmosphere was charged with anticipation. The stadium buzzed with energy, fans eagerly waiting to see this promising teenager take the field. As Pelé stepped onto the grass, he could feel the world resting on his young shoulders. Nerves and excitement raced through him. What would it feel like to be in front of a crowd that believed in him? To embody the dreams he had chased through countless afternoons filled with dust and sweat?

Then came the moment when he had a chance to score. The ball rolled toward him like a familiar friend, begging for his attention. Time seemed to slow down as he focused, imagining the net ripple and the cheers erupting. With a quick kick, Pelé sent the ball flying into the back of the net. In that instant, the crowd exploded. It was a beautiful mix of joy, disbelief, and celebration.

That first professional goal was more than just a number; it was an outpouring of emotions. Joy, yes, but also something deeper—a sense of accomplishment. The realization that his childhood dreams were starting to come true washed over him like a wave. He would later reflect, "Everything is possible," highlighting the power of dedication and focus. This moment validated all the sacrifices he had made, rewarding him for the years spent perfecting his craft and chasing after what seemed impossible.

But it wasn't just a fairy tale filled with fireworks and applause. The pressures of being in the spotlight weighed heavily on Pelé. Expectations grew, and doubts began to creep in. Could he keep up that success? Would the sparks of brilliance he showed on that unforgettable day fade away under the weight of responsibility? Questions swirled in his mind, but in the midst of all this chaos, he found comfort in his training.

Those early mornings became sacred spaces for him, where he could push aside the doubts and focus on improving. The sacrifices loomed large; Pelé had moved to Santos, leaving his family behind in Bauru. He often thought of them, their faces reminding him of why he pushed himself so hard. The distance wasn't easy, but it fueled his determination to make every moment count, turning that separation into motivation.

He threw himself into intense training sessions, battling through exhaustion with a relentless spirit. Each drop of sweat was a promise made to his family, his coaches, and most importantly, to himself. Pelé understood that achieving greatness required more than just talent; it demanded resilience, dedication, and the willingness to make sacrifices for the dreams you hold dear.

Imagine being in his shoes: young, talented, and suddenly at the center of something bigger than yourself. What sacrifices would you be willing to make for your dreams? It's a question worth considering, as every aspiring champion faces their own turning points. Each challenge becomes a fork in the road, and the choices made there shape the story of one's journey.

During those crucial years, Pelé developed a mindset focused on his goals. Whenever things felt overwhelming, he reminded himself why he played: the love of the game. He found joy in simply kicking the ball, a welcome break from the pressures of being the teenage champion everyone had their eyes on. This connection to his passion became a lifeline, grounding him amidst swirling expectations. He often told himself,

"When you play with your heart, everything else falls into place."

Looking back at his journey, it's clear that Pelé's rise was about more than just talent; it was also about mental strength. His ability to turn pressure into motivation, to transform expectations into fuel for his passion, set him apart. He faced challenges head-on, always pushing against the limits that tried to hold him back.

As he thrived with Santos, Pelé didn't just sharpen his skills; he also learned to navigate the tricky world of professional sports. Media scrutiny, fan expectations, and tough competition were all part of the deal. But instead of feeling overwhelmed, he took on the challenge, becoming a strong player on the field. With each game, he improved, adapting to the fast-paced nature of professional play while staying true to his roots.

He became a beacon of inspiration, not just through his performance but also through his tireless work ethic. Stories of his dedication spread, and soon young players began to look up to him. Pelé had unwittingly turned into a role model, proving to the world that dreams are built on hard work and perseverance.

Every match became a stage for him to showcase his talent, and with each goal he scored, he carved his name deeper into the history of soccer. The cheers from the crowd—the roar of approval—became a soundtrack that pushed him to go further, fueling his ambition. It was about more than just winning; it was about leaving a mark, showing young dreamers everywhere that with enough effort, anything is possible.

As Pelé's star continued to shine, it became clear that he was more than just a teenage sensation. He was a symbol of hope and determination for countless others who dared to dream. His story encourages all of us to think about our own goals: How do you stay on track when things get tough? The answer lies in remembering your passion, clinging to the joy that sparked your dreams in the first place.

In those moments of uncertainty, let Pelé's journey remind you of how a boy with a grapefruit became a teenage champion lighting up stadiums. His unwavering spirit, driven by sacrifice and hard work, shows us that the road to greatness is often filled with obstacles. True champions are born through resilience and a strong belief in oneself.

The world of soccer welcomed Pelé with open arms, but it was his grit and heart that allowed him to thrive. For every young reader dreaming of their future, his story shines as a beacon of hope, reminding us that while the journey may be long, with determination and passion, anything can be achieved. In the grand game of life, the most powerful shot isn't just the one that finds the net but the one that comes from deep inside—the belief that, against all odds, you too can be a champion.

A Legacy That Lives On

Pelé's journey through soccer turned him into a global icon, and every goal he scored helped to build a legacy that would inspire countless others. Winning three FIFA World Cups is no small achievement, yet for Pelé, it was just one chapter in a much larger story—a story filled with resilience, dedication, and an unwavering love for the game. He didn't just play soccer; he transformed it into something extraordinary—a captivating dance that drew in millions.

As the ball soared across the pitch, Pelé commanded it like a conductor leading a symphony, leaving fans in sheer awe. His unique style, a blend of speed, agility, and skill, made every match feel like an unforgettable event. He wasn't just scoring goals; he was crafting moments that would remain in the hearts of soccer lovers for generations. Pelé's artistry on the field changed what it meant to be a soccer player. Every dribble, pass, and shot showcased his passion, motivating young dreamers to tie their shoelaces and step onto the field with hopes of following in his footsteps.

But Pelé's influence went beyond his remarkable skills. He brought a sense of hope and possibility to a sport that unites people from every corner of the globe. The thrill of the World Cup blended beautifully with the joy of a local game, showing us that soccer is not just a game; it's a universal language that speaks to everyone, no matter where they're from. Pelé became the voice of that language, bridging cultures and communities. When he played, people from diverse backgrounds found common ground in their shared love for the sport, reminding us of how powerful sports can be in bringing us together.

What makes Pelé's legacy even more impressive is how he understood the responsibilities that came with his fame. Despite reaching incredible heights, he never forgot his roots. Growing up in poverty, he knew firsthand the struggles faced by many. This understanding fueled his passion for giving back to his community. Pelé was not just a champion on the field; he was also a voice for social change. He recognized that his fame offered him a platform to help others, and he took that responsibility seriously.

Through various charitable efforts, Pelé championed important causes like education, health, and poverty relief. His work in these areas showed that true greatness isn't measured solely by trophies and accolades. He believed in using his influence to uplift those around him, encouraging a generation to take action for the greater good. Pelé's kindness and compassion echoed just as loudly as his skills on the soccer field.

Pelé once said, "I don't believe in legends. I believe in the people." This belief drove him to dedicate time and resources to support initiatives aimed at improving the lives of those less fortunate. He worked with organizations to provide educational opportunities, health services, and support for underprivileged children. Each act of kindness highlighted his commitment to nurturing future generations, proving that a true champion lifts others up, not just themselves.

Pelé's legacy invites us all to think about the kind of impact we want to make in our own lives. How do we want to be remembered? As you explore the incredible stories of legends like Pelé, it's crucial to understand that greatness isn't just about winning; it's also about the positive differences we can make along the way.

In our journey toward our dreams, it's easy to get caught up in personal achievements. But Pelé reminds us that we can also lift others along the way. Each one of us has the power to be a champion, not just in our own fields but also in our communities. We can find ways to contribute, inspire, and create meaningful change in the world.

Imagine being able to impact the lives of others, just as Pelé did. Picture the smiles on children's faces as they learn and grow, supported by someone who believed in them. This is the essence of creating a legacy that endures—one that sparks the light of possibility in others and encourages them to pursue their own dreams. The connection between Pelé's achievements and his philanthropic work illustrates a beautiful truth: champions don't exist alone. Their influence spreads outward, inspiring those around them to dream bigger and work harder.

Throughout his life, Pelé faced numerous challenges, both on and off the field. Each hurdle could have held him back, but instead, he turned them into stepping stones toward greatness. His unwavering determination pushed him forward, teaching us that the road to our dreams is often filled with tests of our will. By learning from our failures and embracing persistence, we too can turn obstacles into opportunities for growth.

Pelé's legacy shows us the power of dreams, hard work, and believing in ourselves. It serves as a strong reminder that anyone can achieve greatness if they're willing to put in the effort and stay committed to their passions.

The spark of inspiration he ignited in others is something that will never fade. It flows through aspiring athletes and everyday people alike, driving their ambitions and encouraging them to push their limits.

As you reflect on Pelé's life, think about the legacy you want to leave behind. What dreams are close to your heart? As you carve out your own path, consider the impact you want to have on those around you. Whether it's shining in a sport, building a career, or making a difference in your community, remember that the choices you make today will shape the stories you share tomorrow.

Let Pelé's life inspire you to aim high, knowing that with hard work, passion, and a commitment to lifting others, you too can create a legacy that lasts. Every step you take, every challenge you encounter, and every dream you chase can contribute to a larger story—one that reflects not just your accomplishments but also the lives you touch along the way.

For young readers, the lessons from Pelé's story remind us of the incredible potential within each of us. He started as a boy with big dreams, grew into a man who achieved great things, and ultimately became a legend whose influence continues to resonate around the world. Let's all strive to carry that torch, lighting the way for others and inspiring future generations to pursue their dreams with the same passion and heart that defined the King of Soccer.

W. Bo Cricklewood

Chapter 5: The Innovator: Johan Cruyff Revolutionizes Soccer

The Birth of the Cruyff Turn

During an intense match, the atmosphere was charged as Johan Cruyff found himself cornered. The stadium buzzed with the excited shouts of fans, their hearts pounding in rhythm with the action on the field. It was 1974, a critical year in soccer history, and the pressure was on as the Dutch national team faced a tough opponent. Cruyff, tall and slender in his bright orange jersey, felt the weight of expectation. A defender stood right in front of him, blocking his way, while spectators lined the sidelines, all eyes glued to him, their hopes resting squarely on his shoulders.

As the clock ticked down, sweat dripped from his forehead, momentarily blurring his vision. But Johan was not one to give up easily. His mind raced, looking for a way out, as quickly as his legs could move. The crowd was a whirlwind of noise, and time seemed to slow down as the defender lunged toward him, arms reaching out, ready to snatch the ball away. In that split second, everything he had practiced clicked into place, and an idea sparked in his mind—one that would transform the game forever.

With a flash of brilliance and a dash of courage, Johan Cruyff performed what would be known as the Cruyff Turn. With a swift flick of his foot, he pulled the ball back, spun on his heel, and elegantly moved away from the defender. The crowd gasped, the sound rippling through the stadium like a wave of electricity. The defender, completely surprised, stumbled past Johan, who glided into open space, leaving only a memory of his incredible agility. It was a magical moment, destined to be remembered in the history of soccer.

The Cruyff Turn is simple yet stunning, a true display of creativity. To pull off this move, you start by approaching the ball, pretending to go one way. As the defender reacts, you quickly drag the ball back with one foot while pivoting on the other, spinning away from your opponent. It's almost like dancing—a beautiful ballet on the soccer field. For those young readers eager to give it a try, picture yourself playfully tricking a sibling or friend, making them think you'll go one way, then surprising them with a quick twist in another direction.

Practicing this move can feel empowering. Imagine standing on a grassy field, the soccer ball at your feet, and the sun warming your back. You gather your energy, take a deep breath, and execute the turn. There's something thrilling about transforming from a nervous beginner into a player who can make defenders second-guess their every move.

But Johan Cruyff's invention didn't just confuse opponents; it became a go-to move for soccer players everywhere, from local teams to professional leagues. Young players across the globe started to master the turn, each adding their own twist, capturing a bit of Cruyff's magic in their style of play. Legendary players like Lionel Messi and Cristiano Ronaldo have pointed to Johan's creativity as a significant influence on their own careers, showing how one person's genius can inspire many. Cruyff's vision didn't just change how players dribbled;

it opened the door for creativity and innovation to flourish in every match.

The impact of the Cruyff Turn also offers a valuable lesson for life: thinking outside the box is key. There will be times when it feels like the world is closing in, and solutions seem just out of reach. But like Johan, embracing creativity and adaptability is often the best way forward. Whether you're dealing with challenges in soccer, school, or life, every hurdle can be a chance to rethink your approach.

Think about those times you had to find a clever solution. Maybe it was during a game when you needed to outsmart an opponent or in school when a tricky math problem called for a fresh perspective. Just as Johan showed us on that historic day, being flexible and open to new ideas can lead to amazing results.

Whenever you spot a player pulling off the Cruyff Turn, remember that it all started with one person who dared to trust his instincts. It serves as a reminder that, much like soccer, life is full of unexpected twists, and the best players—both on the field and in life—are those who can adapt and face change with creativity and confidence. So, as you lace up your shoes and head to the field, take a moment to imagine what incredible moves you might come up with. Who knows? You might just create the next iconic soccer trick.

Total Soccer Philosophy

Soccer has always been about structure. Before Johan Cruyff entered the picture, players were usually stuck in strict positions. Forwards rushed down the field, midfielders controlled the center, and defenders stood guard near the goal, like watchful protectors. This setup created a predictable game; players rarely ventured beyond their assigned zones. For coaches, this meant a clear understanding of each player's responsibilities, but it also resulted in a lack of creativity and fluidity on the field. While the game could be beautiful, it often felt like a well-rehearsed performance, leaving little space for spontaneity or imagination.

Then came Cruyff, whose fresh ideas turned the game upside down. He questioned the traditional views of soccer, insisting that players shouldn't be stuck in one spot but should instead be flexible, dynamic, and adaptable. He introduced the idea of "Total Football," a groundbreaking shift that would change soccer forever. In this new approach, any player could take on any role at any moment, creating an exciting and unpredictable style of play that kept opponents on their toes.

At Ajax, where Cruyff developed his concepts, training sessions transformed into something special. Imagine a bright day in Amsterdam, where eager young players gathered for practice. As they arrived on the field, they found more than just cones and goals; they discovered a lively classroom of soccer. Cruyff encouraged his players to have fun and laugh, reminding them that enjoying the game was just as important as mastering tactics. One day, during warm-ups, a player joked, "So, are we forwards today or defenders? Maybe we should all wear each other's jerseys!" and the whole group burst into laughter. This lightheartedness became a crucial part of their training, emphasizing that while soccer is serious, it can also be a joyful adventure.

During these sessions, Cruyff introduced challenging drills that focused on seeing the game as a whole rather than a series of individual tasks. Players learned to read the field, anticipate each other's movements, and switch roles in the moment. It wasn't just about knowing where to stand or how to pass; it was about feeling the flow of the game and actively contributing to it. Young players quickly adapted from offense to defense, realizing their true value lay in their flexibility. The laughter echoed through practice, signaling a deeper understanding as players learned to think together rather than as isolated parts of a machine.

The results of this innovative training soon became clear. Matches began to showcase a style that had never been witnessed before. Picture a packed stadium, filled with passionate fans, all holding their breath as Ajax pulled off a stunning series of passes. The ball flew from player to player with a grace that felt almost magical. Cruyff's focus on movement off the ball created spaces that left defenders baffled, unable to guess where the next play would come from.

One unforgettable match captured this approach perfectly. It was a European Cup semifinal, and Ajax faced a tough opponent.

When the whistle blew, Ajax players sprang into action, displaying an intricate dance of movement and teamwork. The ball flowed smoothly, never tethered to one player but moving through the team like an electric current. Johan Cruyff was right at the center of it all, directing the play, smoothly shifting roles as he slipped past defenders. The crowd was mesmerized, witnessing a performance that felt like a beautifully coordinated symphony of soccer where every player played their part in a shared goal.

As the game went on, it became clear that Total Football was more than just a strategy; it was a philosophy that celebrated teamwork. Players positioned themselves, made runs, and communicated in ways that made them look like a single unit rather than a group of individuals. When Ajax scored, it wasn't just a display of skill; it was a powerful demonstration of their connection, proving that together they were greater than the sum of their parts. Fans erupted in cheers, but the players savored the knowledge that they were part of something bigger than themselves.

As this philosophy spread beyond Ajax to FC Barcelona, where Cruyff took the helm as manager, it became ingrained in soccer history. Barcelona turned into a living example of Total Football, winning countless titles and transforming into a soccer powerhouse.

Training sessions echoed the ones at Ajax, with players laughing and experimenting, no longer weighed down by strict positional roles.

The spirit of adaptability reached beyond the field. Think about the lives we lead—whether in sports, school projects, or family gatherings. The lessons from Total Football are relevant for everyone. Just as players learned to embrace flexibility, we too can find success by being open to different roles within our teams. In school, you might remember a group project where one person took the lead, another focused on research, and someone else handled the presentation. The collaboration in those moments often led to the best results, highlighting the power of working together.

Consider your own experiences in team sports. Have you ever had a teammate step in to fill a need, or witnessed someone's adaptability turn a tough situation around? Perhaps there was a day when your soccer team was down a goal, and someone proposed a change in strategy, surprising the other side by switching formations. That could have led to a thrilling comeback, leaving everyone buzzing with excitement from having worked together.

The ability to be flexible and recognize others' strengths is vital, whether you're on the field or working on a school project. The essence of Total Football is evident not only in the performances of elite athletes but also in the everyday lives of young people eager to learn and grow. The best teams, just like the best friendships, flourish through mutual understanding and adaptability.

Through Cruyff's philosophy, we gain a guide to success that goes beyond soccer. Being flexible and ready to tackle new challenges can lead to remarkable achievements. When we open ourselves up to understanding each other's strengths and weaknesses, we not only enhance our individual skills but also uplift the team spirit. Just like the players who mastered Total Football, we all have the potential to create something extraordinary when we embrace change and celebrate working together.

The legacy of Total Football continues to inspire generations of players and fans. In a world that often pressures us to fit into predefined molds, Cruyff's vision invites us to break free, explore, and redefine how we collaborate. So the next time you step onto the field or find yourself in a group, remember the magic of adaptability. Who knows what incredible moments can happen when we're willing to take on new roles and let the game flow around us?

Breaking the Mold: The Legend of Number 14

In the world of sports, there are moments that change everything we thought we knew. For Johan Cruyff, that pivotal moment came when he decided to wear the number 14 jersey. At first glance, this may seem like a simple choice, but it was actually a game-changing decision that broke the mold in soccer. It opened the door to individuality and self-expression on the field. Suddenly, jersey numbers evolved from just a way to indicate a player's position to something much more personal—a canvas for creativity and identity.

Cruyff didn't choose the number 14 just to stand out—though he certainly did that. His decision was a powerful statement about how he saw the game. In the past, players typically wore numbers that matched their roles: goalkeepers were 1, defenders wore numbers like 2 and 3, midfielders wore 6 to 8, and forwards took numbers 9 and 10. These numbers reflected a strict hierarchy and responsibility. But Cruyff turned this idea upside down. He took the number 14 and filled it with meaning that went way beyond a player's position, transforming it into a symbol of his own identity as both a player and a thinker.

Wearing the number 14 became a badge of honor, declaring to the world that soccer was not only about strict positions and rules, but also about individual flair, creativity, and innovation. As Cruyff raced down the field, that number was like a shadow, reminding everyone that soccer could be played with imagination and artistry. It felt as if he wore a cape instead of a jersey—allowing him to soar above defenders and express his deep love for the game.

The impact of Cruyff's choice was nothing less than revolutionary. In a sport often bound by tradition and expectations, his number 14 inspired countless players to think outside the box. Suddenly, it was perfectly acceptable to be unique, to take risks, and to carve out your own identity on the field. This shift opened doors for young players who had previously felt trapped by the idea of fitting into a mold. Cruyff showed them that they could challenge the norm, embrace their differences, and still thrive in the beautiful game.

Think for a moment about the players who followed in Cruyff's footsteps. Take Roberto Baggio, who wore number 10 but changed what that number represented, or more modern stars like Neymar, who took to the pitch with number 11, showcasing flair and charisma. Each of these athletes embraced their own style and identity, using their numbers to express who they were. Even more importantly, they carried on the legacy of individuality that Cruyff sparked decades earlier.

Today, you can see Cruyff's influence in players who wear numbers that once would have seemed impossible. A midfielder sporting the number 7, a goalkeeper confidently wearing 9, or a forward choosing 6—these choices are a clear nod to the legacy Cruyff created. They represent a growing acceptance of individuality in soccer, encouraging players to redefine themselves beyond traditional roles. A jersey number is no longer just a label; it has become a part of who they are.

This shift in how jersey numbers are viewed mirrors a larger movement toward celebrating uniqueness, not just in soccer, but in life as well. The idea that everyone has special qualities worthy of recognition is an important lesson for young athletes and fans alike. It shows that embracing your individuality isn't just okay—it can lead to incredible success and happiness.

Take a moment to consider what it means to show your true self. Whether on the soccer field or in everyday life, each of us has unique traits that shape who we are. For some, it might mean a knack for creative problem-solving, while for others, it might be a talent for rallying teammates or coming up with clever strategies during a game. Just like Cruyff boldly wore number 14 and carved his own path, everyone is encouraged to explore their own identity and celebrate it with pride.

As we think about these ideas, it's fascinating to see how self-expression can appear in many forms. Can you remember a time when you took a risk, whether in sports or at school? Maybe you tried out for a position you had never played before or shared a unique idea in class. The thrill of being true to yourself can be both exciting and life-changing. Just like Cruyff weaving through defenders with the ball, you too can find joy in breaking away from expectations.

Johan Cruyff's journey reminds us of the power of individuality, especially in places that might feel strict or traditional. Each person has their own set of strengths and talents, and embracing those differences can empower us to do great things. Cruyff didn't just change soccer; he opened up new possibilities for generations of players, encouraging them to break free from conventional thinking.

The legacy of Cruyff's number 14 continues to inspire young athletes to take pride in who they are and to push their limits. In a world where fitting in can often feel like the easy route, it's more important than ever to recognize the value of being different. We are all unique in our ways, and that diversity enriches our teams and communities.

As we move through life, let's draw inspiration from Cruyff's spirit. Embracing our unique qualities and expressing them can lead to amazing outcomes. Whether you find yourself on the soccer field, in a classroom, or with friends, take a moment to think about how you can honor your individuality. Like Cruyff, don't hesitate to take risks and show the brilliance that comes from being true to yourself. Each of us has a unique story to tell, and the world deserves to hear it. So, let's celebrate the number 14—not just as a jersey, but as a powerful reminder to be bold, be different, and cherish the beauty of our individuality.

Chapter 6: Miracle Comeback: Liverpool's Night of Triumph

Never Give Up

As the teams walked off the field and into the dim confines of the locker room, a heavy silence wrapped around the Liverpool players. The cheers from the Atatürk Olympic Stadium faded, replaced by the echo of the referee's whistle and the stark awareness of their tough situation. Three goals down in a Champions League final—how could anything feel more overwhelming? The weight of expectations bore down on them, the dreams of countless fans resting on their shoulders, and yet, in that moment, it felt like everything was slipping away.

Steven Gerrard, the heart of Liverpool, sat slumped on a bench, a picture of despair. His teammates looked just as defeated; the fire in their eyes had faded to mere embers as they faced the harsh reality of their predicament. It felt as if the weight of history was pressing down on them, the legacy of past victories starkly contrasting the bitter taste of defeat that loomed. Still, amidst the gloom, a spark flickered in Gerrard's mind. This was not how the story would end—not tonight.

Raising his head, he scanned the room. The air was thick with disappointment, but he sensed something deeper—a potential waiting to be tapped into. He was more than just a captain; he had an incredible gift for lifting those around him. In moments like this, leadership meant more than strategies and formations; it transformed into a powerful call to arms.

"Hey, listen up," he said, his voice cutting through the heavy atmosphere. "This isn't over. Not by a long shot. We're Liverpool Football Club, and we don't back down." His words were filled with a passion that broke through the fog of despair. Some players lifted their heads, curiosity sparked; others remained lost in thought. But Gerrard knew he had to shake them awake. "We can't change what's already happened, but we can change what's about to happen. We're going to fight, and we're going to make our fans proud."

His passionate speech created a ripple effect. He could see the flickers of determination lighting up in his teammates' eyes. "One goal at a time," he urged, his confidence unwavering. "Let's get back out there and show them what we're made of."

Gerrard's spirit was contagious. The room shifted from resignation to a fragile but growing resolve. They weren't just down by three; they were still alive and capable of turning the game around. They were players forged by challenges, shaped by fire, ready to charge back into the fray.

As the second half approached, thoughts started to solidify. The careful notes, strategies, and plays that had been discussed before the match faded from memory. The focus shifted from meticulous planning to the raw emotion and passion that Liverpool represented. There was no denying AC Milan's skill, but they needed to remember that football is ultimately a game driven by the human spirit.

The players stepped back onto the pitch, their hearts pounding with renewed energy and their eyes shining with determination to take control of their fate. The contrast between the two teams was striking.

Liverpool stood strong, embodying the fierce spirit of their city, while AC Milan seemed composed and confident, relishing the comfort of their seemingly unassailable lead.

As the whistle blew to kick off the second half, Gerrard's eyes locked onto the ball. Liverpool needed to set the tone right away; they had to make their mark before time slipped away. A sense of urgency crackled among the players, each one fueled by the belief that they could claw their way back into the match.

In the opening minutes, Liverpool surged forward with a passion that had been missing in the first half. They pressed AC Milan hard, forcing them back, and while every Liverpool fan in the stadium held their breath, the players began to connect, passing the ball fluidly as if awakening from a deep slumber. The fans, now sensing that their team was fighting back, erupted into a wave of cheers, singing and shouting with a passion that shook the very ground beneath them.

And then it happened. A flicker of hope appeared in the form of a goal. This wasn't just any goal; it was a statement to the world that they wouldn't fade away quietly. Gerrard leaped into the air to meet a corner with an electrifying header that smashed into the net. The roar of the crowd was deafening, sending chills down the spines of everyone fortunate enough to witness it. Just like that, they were back in the game.

"Come on!" Gerrard shouted, his voice cutting through the joyful chaos around him. "Let's get another!" A wave of belief surged through Liverpool, like a powerful jolt of energy. There was still a steep climb ahead, but that one moment had started their ascent.

As the clock ticked on, the momentum shifted. Liverpool, fueled by their captain's infectious spirit and the unyielding support of their fans, pushed forward with renewed strength. Their hunger for more was palpable; each pass, each tackle, and every moment on the ball was filled with purpose. AC Milan looked rattled; the confidence they had in the first half began to wane, and cracks in their defenses became visible.

Another goal came quickly—a fierce effort that brought the score to 3-2. This wasn't just a comeback; it was a storm brewing. The realization dawned that Liverpool might just snatch victory from the jaws of defeat. The stadium exploded in cheers as fans sang louder than ever, their voices a beautiful blend that drowned out any lingering doubts.

As the game neared its climax, Liverpool had not only clawed back two goals; they were now a force to be reckoned with. AC Milan looked increasingly shaky, their earlier confidence crumbling under the relentless pressure from their opponents. Gerrard, now a whirlwind on the field, embodied Liverpool's resurgence—a shining beacon of hope and determination that his teammates rallied around.

The dramatic second half reached its peak when, in the final moments, Liverpool pulled off a play that would be remembered in football history. The ball found its way to a teammate waiting in the box, and with a deft touch, he drove it past the Milan goalkeeper, completing a breathtaking comeback. The stadium erupted once again, this time in pure joy, as the score stood at 3-3.

Liverpool had rewritten their narrative in the most thrilling way. They had not just refused to lose; they had inspired their fans and shown that they possessed a fierce spirit that couldn't be broken. As they prepared for the final moments of the match, it was clear that the stage was set for an unforgettable showdown—one that would be remembered for years to come.

This was about so much more than the score; it was about a mindset—a determination not to accept defeat. The powerful lesson resonated in the hearts of players and fans alike: resilience can change everything. Liverpool had clawed their way back from the brink, embodying the truth that greatness is often forged in the fires of hardship. The world was watching, and it was becoming evident that this night would be remembered not just for the final score, but for the unwavering belief that transformed despair into triumph.

Never Give Up

As the Liverpool players gathered in the locker room, a heavy silence hung in the air. It felt like time had paused, trapping them in a bubble of uncertainty and worry. They had stepped onto the pitch as underdogs, and now they found themselves three goals down in the UEFA Champions League final. The cheers from the AC Milan fans echoed in their ears, a constant reminder of the huge challenge ahead. Desperation threatened to swallow them, and the dreams of countless supporters felt far out of reach.

In the middle of this storm of emotions stood Steven Gerrard, a figure known for his passion and unyielding spirit. His shoulders drooped as he looked around the room, taking in the weight of the moment. For a captain, it's not just about strategy or skills; it's about igniting a spark in the hearts of your teammates. Gerrard understood that the time to act was now; they needed to turn the pressure into motivation.

He rose to his feet, taking a moment to steady himself. His eyes, usually ablaze with fierce determination, now shone with an intensity that demanded their attention. "Hey, listen up," he began, his voice cutting through the thick silence. "This isn't over. Not even close. We're Liverpool Football Club, and we don't back down."

Gerrard's words sliced through the gloom, making even the most disheartened players sit up and pay attention. The silence that had weighed them down began to lift, replaced by a flicker of curiosity. Gerrard pressed on, his voice growing stronger with every word. "We can't change what's happened, but we can change what's about to happen. We're going to fight, and we're going to make our fans proud."

With those heartfelt declarations, a spark of hope ignited in the room. The collective sigh of despair slowly transformed into a steely determination, and Gerrard could sense the shift; he saw it reflected in his teammates' eyes. The idea of a comeback, no matter how far-fetched it seemed, began to take root. "One goal at a time," he urged, his confidence unwavering. "Let's get back out there and show them what we're made of."

As they walked out of the locker room, the mood had shifted from defeat to renewed energy. The players stepped onto the pitch with their heads held high. Gerrard had reignited something essential—the spirit of being a Liverpool player. They weren't just a team facing defeat; they were warriors filled with the belief that anything was possible.

When the second half began, the pace picked up immediately. Liverpool charged forward with a fire that had been missing in the first half. The players began to connect, their movements fluid and synchronized, as if they were suddenly driven by an invisible force. With each pass, they wove a story of defiance and passion. The AC Milan players, who had seemed so invincible before, now felt the tremors of doubt.

A defining moment arrived when none other than Steven Gerrard scored a goal. He soared above the defenders like a hawk, meeting the corner kick with a powerful header that thundered into the net. The Atatürk Olympic Stadium erupted into joyful chaos, a blend of cheers and shouts. Energy surged through Liverpool's players like electricity, and the roar of the crowd fueled their determination. "Come on!" Gerrard shouted, his voice ringing out amid the joyous uproar. "Let's get another!"

The momentum had shifted; belief flowed through Liverpool like a fresh surge of energy. Each pass was sharper, each tackle more purposeful. The confidence that had slipped away began to return, and with every touch of the ball, they moved closer to the unbelievable.

Then, in response to their newfound drive, another goal came quickly. A beautiful sequence of play ended with a strike that rocketed past the Milan goalkeeper. The score was now 3-2, and the electric atmosphere thrummed with the thrill of possibility. The realization that they could achieve the impossible stoked their fire even further. The stadium buzzed with excitement, a chorus of shared hope resonating in every corner.

As the game approached its final moments, Liverpool transformed into a team reborn. They had not just bounced back from despair; they had evolved into a united force with unwavering purpose. Gerrard became a whirlwind on the field, embodying the relentless spirit of the club. The AC Milan players, once dominant, now appeared vulnerable, their confidence cracking under the relentless pressure.

The climax of the match was nearing, and with it came a moment that would be remembered in football history. As the clock ticked down, Liverpool executed a flawlessly coordinated attack. The ball reached a teammate in the box, and with a swift touch, it slid past the helpless goalkeeper, leveling the score at 3-3. The stadium exploded in an outburst of joy, a celebration that words couldn't capture.

This moment was more than just a score. It was a powerful testament to resilience, showcasing a mindset that refused to accept defeat. The crowd, a sea of red, celebrated not just a comeback but a shining example of the unbreakable spirit that defines football. Liverpool had risen from the ashes, transforming what could have been a night of despair into a celebration of hope and triumph.

The lessons from this remarkable match were clear and resonated deeply with players and fans alike. Greatness often springs from struggle; champions are not defined by their setbacks but by their determination to rise again. Liverpool had demonstrated to the world that with belief and tenacity, even the toughest challenges can be met with unshakeable spirit.

Victory Against All Odds

The roar of the crowd echoed through the Atatürk Olympic Stadium, a mix of sounds that blended hope, desperation, and disbelief. Liverpool had battled their way back to tie the score at 3-3, an achievement that seemed impossible just moments before. The journey from despair to this thrilling moment was truly miraculous. As the final minutes of the match ticked away, the atmosphere buzzed with an energy that resonated in the hearts of every player on the field and every fan in the stands.

For Liverpool, this was no longer just a game; it was a rallying cry. The players felt the rhythm of the stadium in their bones, the chants rising higher and higher, filling the air with songs of hope and unity. "You'll Never Walk Alone" floated through the crowd, a powerful anthem of resilience that seemed to weave itself into their very spirit. They weren't just trying to save a match; they were redefining what it meant to be Liverpool.

In that charged moment, Jerzy Dudek, Liverpool's goalkeeper, became the center of attention. His role in the net was more than just stopping shots; it symbolized hope itself. Each save he made reflected the unwavering spirit of the entire team. The world watched as

Dudek transformed uncertainty into determination. With penalties looming, he had to dig deep and summon all the courage and skill he had.

As the match clock wound down, time felt like it had frozen. Liverpool's momentum surged with a force that seemed almost otherworldly. They pressed on, every player working together with a shared purpose, their eyes fixed on victory. Gerrard, filled with a newfound sense of destiny, led the charge. "One more!" he yelled, rallying his teammates like a general leading his troops into battle. Every pass was sharp, every movement intentional, as they combined their will into a powerful force of determination.

Then came the moment that would make this match legendary. In the dying seconds, the ball flew into the box, a perfectly placed pass slicing through the Milan defense. A Liverpool player was right where he needed to be, and with a swift touch, he sent the ball soaring past the stunned goalkeeper. The stadium erupted into a frenzy. The score was now tied at 3-3, and it felt as if time itself had exploded with joy.

What followed was pure chaos. Liverpool fans jumped to their feet, hands raised high, tears of joy mixing with shouts of disbelief. Strangers hugged, a wave of red and white as passionate as the players on the field.

The players, too, lost themselves in the moment, caught up in a whirlwind of limbs and laughter, the sheer joy of achievement flowing through them like an electric current. This was not just a comeback; it was a resurrection.

The whistle blew, signaling the end of regular time and sending the teams into a penalty shootout. The tension in the air was thick, a living entity that wrapped around each spectator and player alike. With every heartbeat, the collective anxiety rose, but within the Liverpool camp, there was a strong belief that they could conquer this final challenge. After all they had experienced—the highs and lows—how could they not feel that fate was on their side?

As the penalty shootout began, every kick became a crucial moment, a testament to the spirit of the team. Milan took the first kick, and with that initial strike, the pressure mounted. But as the ball sailed past the post, a collective gasp escaped from the Liverpool fans, quickly followed by a wave of confidence. Jerzy Dudek, in his goal, became the embodiment of determination, setting the stage for the kicks that followed.

When it was Liverpool's turn, the players stepped up with an aura of confidence. Each kick was executed flawlessly, the ball finding the net as if drawn there by an unseen force. Dudek's resolve grew stronger with every save he made, turning the shootout into his showcase of heroics. The moment that became etched in history was when he dove dramatically to his left, stretching through the air to stop a Milan penalty. Time slowed, each second stretching into forever, as the ball hung in the air before crashing into Dudek's outstretched hand.

In that moment, he became a hero not just to his teammates, but to every single fan who believed that this night was meant to be theirs. The stadium erupted in cheers, a wave of jubilation that washed over Dudek like a tidal wave. The celebration reached a fever pitch, every face in the stands reflecting the joy of hope fulfilled. The impossible had turned into reality.

With each subsequent kick, the pressure only intensified, but Liverpool's belief never faltered. They moved forward with determination, their collective spirit guiding them. As the final penalty was taken and the ball again found the back of the net, the truth of their victory began to sink in. Liverpool had triumphed against all odds, an achievement that would be cherished for generations.

In the midst of the joyful chaos, the trophy awaited. Liverpool players embraced one another, a wave of camaraderie swelling inside them. They had done this together, every pass, every tackle, every moment of doubt leading to the ultimate reward. Lifting the UEFA Champions League trophy high above their heads, they became symbols of hope and perseverance. The night was a vivid reminder of how passion, unity, and hard work can turn even the direst situations around.

As confetti fell like a gentle shower, glimmering pieces of triumph raining down on the players, the echoes of that unforgettable night began to resonate through time. This wasn't just a victory for a club; it was a powerful message for anyone willing to listen. The heart of this match lay in its display of teamwork, resilience, and the unshakeable belief that we can rise above our circumstances.

This incredible tale of Liverpool's comeback shows us something meaningful. It reminds us that life, much like soccer, can often feel like a steep climb. Challenges and obstacles may seem overwhelming, but the spirit of perseverance can spark change. It encourages us to tap into our inner strength, to come together when times get tough, and to believe wholeheartedly in the power of hope.

Each of us has the ability to write our own comeback story, to face our trials head-on and turn them into moments of triumph. The spirit of that iconic night can inspire us, urging us to never give up and to confront each challenge with a brave heart. This story is not just a celebration of Liverpool's victory; it invites us to carry the lessons of that night forward, reminding us that as long as we stand together and hold onto hope, we can create our own miracles.

W. Bo Cricklewood

Chapter 7: The Unbelievable Save: Gordon Banks vs. Pelé

An Unstoppable Shot

The 1970 World Cup in Mexico is often celebrated as one of the greatest tournaments in soccer history. Under the blazing sun, teams fought not just for wins, but for the pride of their nations. Among the unforgettable players that year, one name stood out: Pelé. His movements on the field were like poetry, gliding through defenders with a grace that felt almost magical. He wasn't just playing; he was creating art, showcasing the beauty of the game in breathtaking ways. But even the brightest stars have their critics. On that pivotal day in June, Pelé faced his in the form of a goalkeeper—Gordon Banks.

As the clock ticked down in the quarterfinal match between England and Brazil, the atmosphere crackled with excitement. Millions of eyes were glued to the screen, hearts racing in anticipation. Brazil was in the lead, their iconic yellow jerseys alive with energy and flair. But it was Pelé's perfectly timed header that had everyone holding their breath. He soared majestically above the defenders, connecting with the ball in a split-second moment that seemed to unfold in slow motion. It was an extraordinary leap, a dazzling display of athleticism. The net was ready to shake with the impact of his strike.

But just like that, Banks appeared—calm in the storm. What followed is now known as one of the greatest saves in soccer history. With an incredible leap, Banks stretched every muscle, fingertips brushing the ball just enough to send it away from the net. It wasn't just a save; it was a testament to the human spirit, a reminder that sometimes, determination can defy all odds.

The ball flew past the goalposts, leaving fans in utter disbelief. For a heartbeat, the world seemed to pause. The crowd erupted, not just in celebration of the save but in admiration for the skill, bravery, and sheer grit it took to achieve it. In that instant, Banks became a symbol of resilience. He showed that no challenge is too great when faced with courage.

Gordon Banks' path to that unforgettable moment was as inspiring as the save itself. Growing up in the heart of industrial England, he faced his share of hurdles. Born in 1937 into a working-class family, opportunities were often few and far between. But rather than letting his circumstances limit him, Banks turned his love for soccer into motivation. He spent endless hours practicing, honing his skills on the muddy fields of his hometown. Each slip and slide on those fields shaped him into a player with quick reflexes and an unshakeable mindset.

A goalkeeper's role often goes unnoticed, overshadowed by the glitz surrounding forwards and midfielders. Banks recognized this but took pride in his position. He knew that every shot he stopped was a sign of teamwork. A strong defense and a confident goalkeeper were vital for any successful team. With this in mind, he built an incredible bond with his defenders, creating a silent understanding that turned their play into a beautifully choreographed performance.

As time went on, Banks' hard work paid off, leading him to the peak of his career. He joined the English national team and played in the victorious 1966 World Cup. But it was the 1970 World Cup that truly cemented his legacy. The pressure was palpable as he stood ready between the posts, fully aware of the significance of his role. Every save mattered; every goal could mean triumph or heartbreak.

In that legendary match, the clash of Pelé's artistry and Banks' determination created a story that would echo for generations. As Pelé rose to head the ball, everyone understood the weight of that moment. But Banks had different plans. His incredible save became a highlight of the tournament, showcasing not just his talent but the very spirit of sportsmanship. The respect that bloomed between Banks and Pelé surpassed the competitive nature of the match, growing into a lifelong friendship.

Their connection serves as a powerful reminder that even in competition, respect and admiration can thrive. They both understood the immense pressure that came with their positions—one an artist of movement, the other a protector of the goal. After the match, they embraced, symbolizing their mutual recognition of each other's greatness. Banks later reflected, "When I made that save, I didn't just save a goal; I saved a piece of my own history."

The moments that shape us often arise from challenges and setbacks. For young athletes watching today, the message is clear: perseverance isn't just about winning. It's about confronting obstacles with courage, believing in your abilities, and seizing every opportunity. Banks' incredible save is a metaphor for life. We all face moments when it feels like an unstoppable shot is hurtling toward us, with the odds stacked against us. But with focus, determination, and the willingness to face challenges head-on, we too can create our own unforgettable moments.

The magic of that save didn't fade with the final whistle. It lived on in the memories of those who witnessed it, a testament to the unwavering spirit of both the player and the game. The stories of Pelé and Banks continue to inspire, encouraging us to rise above our circumstances and strive for greatness. Their journey reveals a beautiful truth: every obstacle can be overcome when approached with heart, determination, and belief in oneself.

Looking back on Banks' journey, we see the reflections of countless young athletes today. They wrestle with insecurities and fears, navigating the competitive worlds of sports, school, and beyond. Just as Banks faced his share of setbacks, they will also encounter challenges that test their resolve. The important thing to remember is that these defining moments do more than shape careers; they build character.

In the world of soccer, the goalkeeper often stands as the unsung hero, with little recognition. But in that match against Brazil, Banks flipped the script. He transformed a routine save into a breathtaking moment, a piece of magic that would be recounted in classrooms and living rooms for years to come. The impact of that one action extends far beyond the soccer field; it inspires each of us to find our own "unstoppable shot" and rise to the occasion, no matter how daunting the odds may seem.

Ultimately, the relationship between Pelé and Banks showcases a deeper understanding of what competition truly means. It's not just about the trophies or fame; it's about the bonds we create, the respect we earn, and the lasting impressions we leave on each other's lives. The beautiful game has the power to unite even the fiercest rivals in a shared celebration of human potential.

And so, as the echoes of the crowd fade into history, the spirit of that moment remains alive. It reminds us that in the game of life, we all have the chance to make an unbelievable save, to beat the odds, and to build a legacy that inspires those who follow. Whether on the field or in our daily lives, the desire to overcome challenges is something we all share. Let's carry that lesson with us, knowing that every challenge we face is just another opportunity to score our own goals.

The Impossible Defended

In the world of sports, some moments stick with us, becoming legends that echo through time. Picture the year 1970, in Mexico, where soccer fans held their breath as England faced Brazil in the quarterfinals of the World Cup. On one side was Pelé, the legendary forward known for his incredible ability to dance around defenders with a grace that seemed almost magical. On the other side was Gordon Banks, the goalkeeper famous for making unbelievable saves look easy. But no one could have predicted the astonishing scene that would unfold as Pelé soared high, and Banks reached even higher.

The atmosphere was electric. As Pelé made his move, you could feel the crowd collectively hold its breath, sensing something extraordinary about to happen. Time seemed to slow down as Pelé leaped into the air, meeting the ball with pinpoint accuracy, directing it toward the net like a divine act. The goal was just moments away, seemingly destined to secure Brazil's victory. But fate had a different plan, and it wore gloves.

In an instant, something incredible happened. Banks defied all expectations and gravity itself. It was as if he had an unspoken connection to the ball's path, a sixth sense that kicked in just at the right moment. With reflexes like a cat, he twisted mid-air, arms reaching out, his fingertips brushing the ball just enough to change its direction. What should have been a surefire goal was miraculously tipped over the crossbar. A wave of disbelief swept through the stadium, matched by gasps from viewers around the world. How had he done that?

That remarkable save became a turning point, not just in that match but in the entire history of soccer. Fans and commentators alike would wonder, "Was that magic? Was that skill?" It encapsulated the spirit of determination and athletic prowess. Banks wasn't just stopping a goal; he was sending a message to the world: With hard work and talent, anything is possible.

Gordon Banks' journey to that moment was filled with challenges and hard work. Born in 1937 in the working-class town of Sheffield, his childhood was shaped by the struggles of post-war England. Instead of seeing his situation as a setback, Banks turned his passion for soccer into motivation. He spent countless hours on muddy fields, honing his skills. Every save and every dive taught him the value of dedication and perseverance.

Unlike the flashy forwards who thrived in the spotlight, Banks found beauty in being a goalkeeper. Often overlooked, much like an unsung hero in a story, he knew just how crucial his role was to the game. With each save, he built a connection with his defenders, forming a silent agreement that elevated their teamwork to remarkable levels. This understanding became a key part of his success, earning him unwavering trust from his teammates. They knew that when the pressure was on, Banks was their rock.

By the time the 1970 World Cup arrived, Banks was already well-known. He had played a crucial role in England's victorious 1966 World Cup run. With every match, he gained more respect and recognition, but the pressure ramped up as he prepared to face Brazil, a team famous for its dazzling style of play. The world was eagerly watching, knowing this would be a clash of titans. The stakes had never been higher, but Banks remained calm. He thrived in high-pressure situations.

When the match kicked off, the excitement in the air was palpable. Fans in bright colors cheered, some rooting for England, others for Brazil, but all united by their love of the beautiful game. As the match went on, the tension thickened. Every pass, every shot at goal had the power to change the game. But when Pelé launched himself for that fateful header, it felt as though time itself was holding its breath.

What followed wasn't just a save; it was a moment that captured the beauty of sport—a clash of two extraordinary talents. As Banks landed from his remarkable leap, the energy shifted. The crowd went from stunned silence to roaring applause, not just for the save, but for the sheer audacity of it all. It reminded everyone that sometimes, the biggest achievements come when facing seemingly impossible odds.

Afterward, Banks and Pelé shared a moment that went beyond competition. Their eyes met in mutual respect, acknowledging each other's greatness. What could have been a fierce rivalry turned into admiration, creating a bond that lasted beyond their careers. They both understood the immense pressure of their roles—one an artist crafting goals, the other a guardian protecting glory. Their embrace after the match became a symbol of camaraderie, showing that respect can thrive even amidst fierce competition.

Reflecting on that incredible moment, Banks later said, "When I made that save, I didn't just save a goal; I saved a piece of my own history." His words resonate with anyone who has faced challenges. It's a testament to the spirit of perseverance—how we can turn obstacles into stepping stones, crafting our own stories through determination and hard work.

This moment offers a valuable lesson for aspiring athletes. Every player faces moments when it feels like an unstoppable shot is coming right at them. Life, much like soccer, is full of challenges that may seem overwhelming. But the message is clear: with focus, determination, and a little courage, the impossible can indeed be defended.

In the realm of sports, the hero isn't always the one who scores the goals. Sometimes, it's the one who stands tall against the odds, guarding the net with unwavering resolve. Banks became that hero in the hearts of fans. His unforgettable save was not just a display of skill; it celebrated the unbreakable spirit that lives in every athlete, reminding them that greatness often appears in the most unexpected places.

That one save echoed through time, inspiring countless young athletes who dream of greatness. They see in Banks a figure who faced adversity, persevered, and emerged victorious. The impossible can become possible when you stay true to your dreams, practice with passion, and commit to your journey.

As time moves forward, the story of Banks and Pelé remains a powerful tale, reminding us that in competition, there's always room for admiration, respect, and friendship. Their bond went beyond the match, embodying the essence of the beautiful game, which unites even the fiercest rivals in mutual respect.

When we think back to that iconic moment in 1970, we're not just recalling a game; we're celebrating the triumph of the human spirit. We remember that every shot on goal can be met with resilience, and that even the most daunting moments can turn into chances for greatness. In our lives, just like on the field, we should face every challenge with the heart of a champion, knowing that every effort can lead to extraordinary results.

The legacy of that save and the friendship between these two giants continues to inspire the next generation of athletes. It

teaches them that in soccer—and beyond—
every challenge we encounter is simply an
opportunity to write our own remarkable
stories, one save at a time. So, let's carry the
spirit of that moment forward, embracing every
chance to stand firm and tackle life's
challenges head-on. Whether we're on the
soccer field or navigating through life's
complexities, we all have the potential to
defend our dreams and become champions of
our own narratives.

A Moment Remembered Forever

As the dust settled on the field in
Mexico, the sounds of cheers and gasps still
hung in the air, transforming the scene into
one of shared appreciation. What began as a
fierce competition between two legendary
figures blossomed into an everlasting
friendship. Gordon Banks, the man who had
beaten the odds, and Pelé, the genius of the
beautiful game, came out of that World Cup
clash as more than just opponents; they
became kindred spirits in the world of sports.

After that incredible save, their
relationship grew, rooted in respect and
friendship. Pelé, with his trademark charm,
often joked about that moment, saying, "How
did you save that? I was already celebrating!"
This playful comment held deeper meaning. It
captured the true spirit of sportsmanship—
showing that competition can thrive without

hostility. It also highlighted a genuine recognition of talent, a shared admiration that rose above the usual rivalries in sports.

These moments remind us that the competitive arena isn't just a battleground; it can also be a place where friendships are formed. Banks and Pelé showed us that even with the high stakes of the game, there's always a chance to appreciate the skills and commitment of others. In a time when athletes often find themselves caught up in personal branding and performance pressures, their story serves as a beautiful reminder that real greatness isn't just about trophies; it's about the bonds we create along the way.

The connection between Banks and Pelé didn't fade when the final whistle blew; instead, it strengthened over the years, showcasing the lasting impact of that one unforgettable moment. Whenever they met at events or reunions, their camaraderie was unmistakable. Their conversations weren't just about their careers but also about how the sport had changed over time, the experiences they shared, and the passion that drove them to the top. They discovered common ground in discussing how the game shaped their lives.

The relationship between Banks and Pelé carries an important message for young athletes. It's crucial to recognize and respect the talents of others, even those who might be in direct competition with us. In a world that often celebrates individual achievements, it can be easy to overlook the skills of those around us. But by acknowledging the strengths of our rivals, we not only enrich our own experience but also create a culture of collaboration instead of conflict.

For the young players watching them compete, the sight of Pelé and Banks sharing a moment of mutual respect should be a source of inspiration. It sends a powerful message: recognizing someone else's talent doesn't take away from your own; it actually makes it shine brighter. Their friendship stands as a testament to the idea that success in sports—and in life— can go hand in hand with respect for others.

Every aspiring athlete dreams of achieving greatness, picturing themselves in the spotlight, lifting trophies, and celebrating victories. Yet, the road to those moments is often filled with challenges. Just like Banks' unforgettable save, the path to success is lined with obstacles that test our determination. The real beauty of this journey lies not just in our triumphs, but also in how we rise to meet the challenges ahead.

In reflecting on his remarkable career, Banks often talked about the value of perseverance. He believed that the desire to improve, learn, and adapt is crucial for any athlete. When asked about the secret behind his incredible save, Banks would point to the countless hours spent training, the sacrifices made, and the lessons learned from every experience. This mindset laid the groundwork for his relationship with Pelé. They both understood that relentless pursuit of excellence is key to succeeding at the highest level, and this shared understanding deepened their bond.

Their friendship reached beyond the soccer field; it became a source of motivation for many. Schools around the world began using their story to show how rivals can turn into allies. They illustrated that, despite the pressures of competition, one can still hold onto integrity and respect. In an era where rivalries can sometimes breed hostility, Banks and Pelé presented a different approach—one marked by admiration and friendship.

In the years following their iconic encounter, the world of soccer underwent significant changes, introducing new challenges and exciting developments. Yet, Banks and Pelé remained devoted to the game, often appearing together at charity events and exhibitions, reminding everyone of their unbreakable bond. Their friendship became a symbol of unity in sports, reinforcing the idea that even the fiercest competition can coexist with camaraderie and respect.

As they grew older, their discussions changed as well. They talked not just about tactics in soccer but also shared valuable life lessons learned on and off the field. Their friendship became a treasure for both men. Young players eagerly gathered to hear their stories, and through them, the values of hard work, dedication, and respect began to spread throughout the soccer community.

The legendary save that gained fame for its audacity was also a starting point for a deeper understanding—the importance of recognizing the humanity in our rivals. Banks' and Pelé's interactions revealed a fundamental truth about competition: while striving for excellence, it's vital to appreciate the effort and talent of those on the other side. This lesson is essential not only for athletes but for anyone facing competition in their lives.

For aspiring players, the echoes of that moment in 1970 should guide them. They remind us that while success matters, the way we treat others in our pursuit of that success is just as important. Pelé and Banks showed us that brilliant moments can lead to lasting connections, and those connections can foster a spirit of unity in a world that often feels divided.

The heart of their friendship teaches us a vital lesson: greatness isn't just about winning awards; it's about the relationships we cultivate along the way. The legacy of that day in Mexico continues to inspire athletes around the world, reminding them that every time they step onto the field, they are part of a much larger story.

As their legacy lives on, the tale of Pelé and Banks serves as a powerful reminder of the potential for respect and admiration to flourish alongside fierce competition. It encourages us to tackle life with the same passion for our craft while also recognizing the efforts of those who share our passions.

Their friendship represents what can happen when we understand that competition doesn't have to create animosity. In sports and beyond, every challenge can become a chance to connect. Every moment on the field can be an opportunity to celebrate the talents of others and enjoy the journey together, regardless of how different our paths may be.

The spirit of that remarkable moment in 1970 still resonates, showing that while the sports world is often filled with rivalries, it can also be a realm of friendships that last a lifetime. With each save, each goal, and each victory, we can choose to honor the spirit of camaraderie that defines our shared love for the game. So, let's remember not just the players and their accomplishments but also the lasting connections that make sports a beautiful story—one that brings us together and encourages us to appreciate the journey we all share in chasing greatness.

W. Bo Cricklewood

Chapter 8: Speed Star: Kylian Mbappé's Rapid Rise

Racing to the Top

Kylian Mbappé's journey starts not in the dazzling stadiums of the world but in a simple neighborhood of Bondy, a town just outside Paris. Imagine a young boy full of energy and dreams, kicking a beat-up soccer ball around with his friends. That boy was Kylian, and from a young age, it was clear he was meant for greatness. Growing up in a family that loved sports, Kylian was more than just another kid who enjoyed soccer; he was a natural talent waiting to shine.

His father, Wilfried, was a soccer coach, teaching Kylian the basics of the game from an early age. There's something truly special about having a parent who knows the ins and outs of a sport—especially one as intricate as soccer. The hours they spent together on the field, the strategy chats at the dinner table, and the encouragement during practices shaped Kylian's understanding of the game. He wasn't just picking up the rules; he was learning about the culture, the beauty, and the relentless drive for excellence that soccer demands.

But it wasn't only his dad who inspired him. His mom, Fayza, a former professional handball player, also played a huge role in Kylian's life. With both parents deeply rooted in athletics, Kylian grew up surrounded by the spirit of competition, resilience, and teamwork. It was a home environment that nurtured ambition and hard work, where effort was not just encouraged but expected. He saw firsthand the sacrifices that come with chasing dreams. Every practice, every game, every setback—these were all lessons Kylian learned to face with remarkable strength.

As Kylian honed his skills, it became clear he was not just another talented kid. His speed was astonishing. He could outrun his friends with an ease that felt almost magical. He moved with a fluidity that belied his age, and while many kids were still learning the basics, Kylian was already pulling off complicated moves that left spectators amazed. There's a certain thrill that fills the air when watching a young talent shine, and those lucky enough to see Kylian in those early years knew they were witnessing something remarkable.

Joining AS Bondy, the local club where his dad coached, was a crucial step in Kylian's early career. The club provided formal training and immersed him in a competitive atmosphere. Here, he learned about teamwork, communication, and collaboration—skills that would serve him well in the future. It was during these important years that Kylian developed a deep love for the game. He trained hard, always pushing himself to improve, to be faster, and to be more skilled.

Picture Kylian, sweat dripping down his face, chasing the ball across the field with an unquenchable thirst for victory. His determination was contagious. It wasn't enough for him just to play; he wanted to be the best. Each drill was a chance to get better, and every game was an opportunity to showcase his growing talent. While other kids might have been satisfied with just playing for fun, Kylian took the game seriously and aimed to make soccer his life. He truly embodied the spirit of a future superstar.

As Kylian's talent began to attract attention, doors to more prestigious clubs opened. Signing with Clairefontaine, the renowned French football academy, was a major turning point in his journey. Known for producing some of the best talents in French soccer history, Clairefontaine became the training ground for Kylian's growth. Surrounded by other gifted athletes all chasing the same dream, he found an even greater drive to push his limits.

Training sessions were tough, yet Kylian faced each challenge with infectious enthusiasm. He quickly realized that achieving success required not only physical skill but also mental strength. Every setback, whether it was a lost game or a moment of doubt, became a chance to learn and grow. He developed a resilience that would become a key part of his character—an ability to bounce back from disappointments with renewed determination and focus.

His desire to be the best wasn't just about ambition; it was fueled by his genuine love for the game. Kylian wasn't just playing for trophies or recognition; he played for the joy it brought him. Soccer was his creative outlet, a place where he could express himself and weave magic. This passion resonated with everyone around him, captivating coaches and teammates alike.

With each passing year, Kylian continued to climb the ranks, dazzling onlookers with his breathtaking speed and technical skills. Scouts from major clubs took notice, and it wasn't long before the legendary Paris Saint-Germain came calling. The chance to join PSG, a team filled with star players, was almost too good to be true. This was his opportunity to shine, to test his skills against the best, and to chase his dream on the grand stage of professional soccer.

However, moving to PSG came with its own set of challenges. The leap from a youth academy to a professional club is like jumping from the shallow end of a pool to the deep end. The competition was tougher, the pressure was higher, and the expectations were immense. Yet, Kylian thrived in this environment. His ability to stay calm, focus on his craft, and keep that childlike love for soccer made him stand out. He was not just another young player; he was Kylian Mbappé, a name that would soon resonate in stadiums around the globe.

As he stepped onto the pitch for his first match with PSG, the energy was electric. Fans were eager to see if this young star could live up to the buzz surrounding him. And as the whistle blew, Kylian didn't disappoint. With every touch of the ball, every sprint down the field, and every goal he scored, he won over the hearts of soccer fans everywhere. His rapid rise was not just due to his exceptional talent; it was a testament to the years of hard work, dedication, and passion that had brought him to this moment.

In those early days with PSG, Kylian became a source of inspiration for young players around the world. He showed that dreams can be reached through perseverance, hard work, and a true commitment to one's passion. Each time he scored, he ignited hope in a new generation, encouraging them to believe in their abilities. Watching him play was like witnessing poetry in motion; he had an amazing knack for dancing through defenders, turning the impossible into reality with breathtaking ease.

As the seasons rolled on, Kylian continued to evolve as a player. Yet, even as he reached incredible heights in his career, he never lost sight of the values his family instilled in him. His roots stayed strong in the humble beginnings of Bondy, a constant reminder of the importance of hard work, dedication, and staying true to oneself. Each victory was celebrated not just as a personal win, but as a tribute to the journey that had brought him there.

Kylian Mbappé's story is a powerful reminder that the path to success is built on determination, resilience, and a passionate pursuit of one's dreams. Through his journey, we see the transformative power of passion and hard work, as well as the vital role of family support. In a world that often emphasizes the end goal, Kylian's rise celebrates the journey itself—filled with lessons that extend far beyond the soccer field.

As he climbed to fame, Kylian Mbappé transformed into not just an incredible athlete but also a role model for young dreamers everywhere. With every swift stride he took on the field, he continued to embody what it truly means to be a champion.

Heart of Gold

Kylian Mbappé isn't just a name known for jaw-dropping talent on the soccer field; it has also come to symbolize generosity and kindness. While his incredible speed and dazzling footwork have captivated fans around the globe, it's his big heart that truly leaves a mark. Winning the FIFA World Cup made him a superstar, but his choice to donate his entire World Cup earnings to charitable causes—especially to help underprivileged children—showed a side of him that often gets lost amid the spotlight of professional sports.

Picture the scene: the sun shining on the trophy, cheers echoing in the background, and there's Kylian, right in the middle, making a decision that would resonate far beyond the soccer field. The news headlines weren't just celebrating his incredible skills that led France to victory; they also praised his selfless act of giving back. It's one thing to be an amazing player; it's a whole different ballgame to use that success to make a positive impact. In that moment, Kylian's generous spirit shone brightly, proving that his heart was just as quick as his feet.

His choice to donate wasn't just a random act of kindness; it was a powerful message. Kylian understood that he was in a special position, with millions watching him. He could inspire change and motivate others to get involved in causes that matter. "I don't think of myself as a superstar. I think of myself as someone who can help," he once said. This quote beautifully captures how he views his role. For Kylian, his journey wasn't just about collecting trophies or seeking personal glory; it was about opening doors for those who haven't yet had their dreams realized.

This urge to lend a helping hand didn't just spring up out of nowhere. It was deeply woven into his upbringing. Growing up in a family that valued sportsmanship, community service, and kindness, Kylian was always conscious of his own privileges and the challenges many others faced. His parents frequently participated in community projects, giving him a solid understanding of how one person can truly make a difference. The lesson was clear: no matter how high you rise, it's essential to remember those who may not have the same opportunities.

Helping underprivileged children became a key part of Kylian's charitable work. But he didn't stop at just making a donation; that was only the beginning. He took the time to visit schools and community centers, spending hours with children who looked up to him, as well as those who needed a little extra encouragement. Each visit turned into a joyful celebration of dreams, where kids got the chance to meet their hero, ask questions, and, most importantly, believe that they too could achieve great things.

There are countless stories about these experiences, painting a vivid picture of Kylian's influence. Imagine a small gym buzzing with laughter and excitement as kids kicked soccer balls, their eyes sparkling with admiration as they tried to mimic Kylian's moves. Each giggle echoed his commitment to showing them that while soccer is thrilling and fun, it's also about teamwork, resilience, and believing in oneself. Kylian would share his own stories—his ups and downs—reminding them that every journey has its bumps along the way.

One child's story, in particular, stood out during one of these outreach events. Young Malik, a shy boy with a love for soccer, had been having a tough time fitting in at school. With every missed goal, his confidence took a hit. When Kylian showed up at a local training session, Malik felt a mix of excitement and nerves. "What if I mess up in front of him?" he worried. But Kylian noticed the potential in Malik, just waiting to be sparked. After practice, he took time to talk with Malik, offering not just words of encouragement but also practical advice. "It's okay to fail; that's how we learn," he reassured the boy, stressing that even the greatest players face setbacks.

By the end of their time together, Malik's face radiated with newfound determination. He walked away believing he could improve, that his dreams were attainable. Kylian's ability to connect with young people and inspire them showed just how impactful his charitable work is. He wasn't just a superstar athlete; he became a mentor, a friend, and a guiding light for those navigating their own paths.

These moments go beyond mere fan encounters; they're lifelines. Kylian's generosity doesn't just touch the lives of children; it inspires fellow athletes and communities too. By setting a strong example, he encourages others in the sports world to use their platforms for good. The effect is remarkable—his actions spark a ripple effect, encouraging more athletes to get involved in charitable work and fostering a culture of giving back in professional sports. Each donation, visit, or community event adds up to something much bigger, showing that the spirit of giving can truly blossom in many hearts.

Kylian's philanthropic work reaches far beyond the soccer field. He partners with organizations focused on education and health, working hard to provide essential resources to those in need. He knows that soccer, while an amazing sport, is just one way to help. It's about tackling bigger issues and pushing for change. By supporting education initiatives, he empowers children with the tools to dream bigger and achieve more, helping them shape their own futures.

His commitment to giving back isn't just a footnote in his incredible career; it's a core part of who he is. As he continues to shine as an athlete, he's also building a legacy as a humanitarian. His lessons on kindness and the importance of community resonate with fans of all ages, encouraging them to think about their own contributions.

Every time Kylian steps onto the field, he carries the weight of expectations—not just to perform like a world-class athlete, but also to be a positive force in the world. That pressure could feel overwhelming, but he approaches it with a sense of responsibility and joy. It's a delicate balancing act, yet he manages it with infectious enthusiasm. "If I can inspire just one child to believe in themselves, I've done my job," he has said. You can feel his dedication to nurturing hope and resilience in the next generation in those words.

Kylian's actions spark a sense of responsibility among his fans and fellow players alike. When you see someone like him—a young superstar achieving so much—choosing to uplift others, it challenges everyone to think about how they can help too. It creates a culture where giving back is the norm, not the exception. Kylian's belief in using his platform for good inspires us all to reflect on our impact on the world around us.

In the end, Kylian Mbappé's story is one that blends talent, hard work, and a strong spirit of generosity. It teaches us that success isn't just about trophies and awards; it's also about the legacy we build through our actions. The kindness we show, the lives we change, and the communities we support—these are the true markers of greatness.

As Kylian continues to amaze fans with his incredible skills on the field, he reminds us all that the heart of a champion is often defined not just by victories, but by the love and kindness shared with others. His journey encourages each of us to think about how we can make a difference in our own communities, inspiring young dreamers everywhere to reach for their potential and spread kindness along the way. This beautiful mix of talent and heart makes Kylian Mbappé not just a soccer star, but a beacon of hope and generosity for the world.

Breaking Records

Kylian Mbappé has turned the world of professional soccer into a stage for remarkable moments, with each match adding a new layer to his incredible story of speed, skill, and amazing accomplishments. The records he's set aren't just statistics; they reflect a journey fueled by passion, hard work, and an unquenchable desire to succeed. While it's tempting to focus solely on the shiny trophies and medals, the real magic comes from understanding what these achievements mean to him personally and to the world of soccer as a whole.

Imagine the scene: the stadium is packed, a colorful sea of excited fans buzzing with energy. The atmosphere is electric as the referee's whistle blows. Every touch of the ball brings Kylian closer to another unforgettable moment. Watching him glide across the field feels almost like poetry in motion, a dynamic blend of energy and focus as he dances around defenders with a natural flair that seems almost unreal. As time ticks away, it's clear that this isn't just another game; it's a moment destined to be etched in memory.

Kylian's journey into professional soccer started with a bang. As a teenager, he quickly became a sensation, making headlines when he became the youngest player to score for AS Monaco in Ligue 1. With that first goal, he didn't just announce his arrival; he sent a message to the entire soccer world. At just 16 years old, he was on a path to greatness, and his career only continued to skyrocket from there. You could almost feel the excitement in the air, and with each flick of his foot, Kylian showed what dedication and hard work can accomplish.

Fast forward to the unforgettable 2018 FIFA World Cup, where he made history as the youngest player since Pelé to score in a World Cup match. That moment wasn't just a personal milestone; it highlighted the immense talent this young star possessed. He played a crucial role in leading France to victory, securing his place in the history books. The joy and disbelief on his face as he celebrated with his teammates were unforgettable. It was a whirlwind of feelings—a victory that felt both deserved and almost dreamlike.

Yet breaking records isn't just about personal glory; it's about the ripple effect it has on a larger scale. Kylian's achievements have sparked inspiration in a new generation of soccer players. In a sport often dominated by seasoned veterans, he stands out as a beacon showing that youth and talent can indeed shake things up. Kids all over the world look up to him, not just as a player but as a symbol of what can be achieved with relentless determination and a strong belief in oneself. His story sends a powerful message: "You, too, can dream big and reach for the stars."

As he continued to shine on the field, Kylian broke through barriers that many thought were impossible. When he transferred to Paris Saint-Germain (PSG), he became the most expensive teenage player in history. The excitement surrounding his arrival was palpable, and he made an immediate impact, scoring goal after goal and setting records that seemed to fall one after another. Whether it was becoming the youngest player to reach a hundred goals in Ligue 1 or making phenomenal contributions in the UEFA Champions League, Kylian wasn't just breaking records; he was rewriting the story of the game.

While numbers can serve as markers in a player's career, they don't tell the entire story. Behind each record is a level of dedication that goes far beyond the game itself. Kylian has faced his share of challenges—injuries, the weight of expectations, and the public scrutiny that comes with fame. Yet through it all, his resilience has shined brightly. He trained harder, refined his skills, and came back stronger. Each setback became a setup for a comeback, reinforcing the idea that success isn't a straight path, but rather a winding road filled with ups and downs.

Beyond the pitch, Kylian's impact extends well beyond just goals and assists. He has become a significant voice in discussions about athletes' responsibilities and their roles in society. His journey has sparked important conversations about using one's platform for good and how records can influence much more than just the game. His actions remind fans and fellow players that sports can drive real change. Kylian's story encourages aspiring athletes everywhere, motivating them to strive for excellence while embracing their role as positive influences.

When we talk about records in soccer, we often think of the breathtaking numbers: the fastest goals, the most assists, and the highest number of goals scored in a season. Kylian has conquered many of these impressive milestones, each time raising the standard even higher. Throughout it all, he has shown gratitude, acknowledging that his success is a team effort involving coaches, teammates, and fans who support him. This humility in the face of acclaim reflects his character, proving that true greatness often comes from collaboration and mutual respect.

Moreover, the chase for records is an ongoing adventure; every milestone reached opens the door for new challenges. For Kylian, the drive to surpass each record comes from a deep-seated passion. He thrives on the thrill of the challenge, constantly pushing the limits of what is possible in the sport. This relentless spirit shines through in his performances, especially when the stakes are high. While the pressure may seem overwhelming to some, for Kylian, it fuels his fire. Each game becomes an opportunity to tell a new story, and with each new chapter, he cements his legacy.

It's worth noting that Kylian's legacy isn't solely about personal records or accolades. It's also about the influence of his accomplishments on his team and the sport itself. Each record he sets inspires not only current players but also those who dream of playing soccer in the future. His journey illustrates that, no matter the obstacles, dreams can be realized through perseverance. His story encourages young players to lace up their boots, hit the fields, and pursue greatness.

As the soccer world continues to change, one thing is clear: Kylian Mbappé's name will be remembered in the annals of soccer history for years to come. He represents a blend of talent and hard work, serving as a reminder that success is often the result of not only individual brilliance but also the backing of a supportive community. While his records may shine brightly, it's the essence of his journey that truly resonates with millions.

In the grand story of soccer, Kylian Mbappé has not only carved out his own chapter; he has opened the door for future stars to dream big and aim high. As fans, we are privileged to witness a phenomenon that challenges the norm, inspiring a spirit of ambition and kindness. With every match, each goal, and every new record, he pushes the boundaries of what it means to be a soccer player today.

The records may mark significant moments in his career, but it's his unwavering dedication to the sport and his generous spirit that will linger most in the hearts of fans. Kylian Mbappé is not just a speedster breaking records; he's a trailblazer redefining what it means to be a champion both on and off the field. As he races toward the future, we can only imagine how many more records he will break, but one thing is certain: he'll pursue them with the same zest, passion, and commitment that has brought him this far. His journey is a powerful reminder of the impact of dreams, determination, and the beautiful game of soccer, inspiring a generation to believe that greatness is within reach for anyone willing to chase it.

W. Bo Cricklewood

Chapter 9: The Secret Weapon: Jens Lehmann's Penalty Masterplan

Homework That Pays Off

Jens Lehmann wasn't just a great athlete; he was also a thinker, a planner, and a strategist. From his early days as a young goalkeeper, he realized that succeeding in soccer took more than quick reflexes and agility. It required thorough preparation, and that's exactly what he did. Lehmann studied his opponents with a focus that could rival any detective.

Imagine him spending countless hours watching game footage—every goal, every missed penalty, and every little move the shooters made. He took detailed notes, breaking down each player's habits and tendencies. He wanted to understand how they approached penalties: Did they take a deep breath before kicking? Did they prefer a specific side of the goal? What cues did their body language give away? By figuring out these questions, he was setting himself up for success long before the match even started.

Lehmann's dedication to his craft was truly remarkable. He didn't just look at the stats; he also dug into the psychology behind each kick. He studied players like Francesco Totti and Roberto Baggio, analyzing their methods and noting the small details that would help him make the right decisions when it really mattered. For him, this wasn't just busywork; it was his secret weapon—a tool that could save games and change the course of crucial moments.

In a world where many young athletes might believe that raw talent is enough, Lehmann's story offers an important lesson: often, it's the preparation done behind the scenes that leads to real success. His notes weren't just filled with names and numbers; they were packed with insights and strategies. He understood that having a sharp mind was just as vital as being physically fit to achieve success on the field.

Think about a moment in his career when he faced a tough opponent in a high-pressure match. As the excitement in the stadium grew and the players lined up for penalties, Lehmann felt a wave of calm confidence wash over him. Why? Because he had put in the work. He recalled how this particular player liked to shoot to the left, a tendency he had identified during his careful film study. As the ball rolled toward him, Lehmann dove in the right direction, pulling off a fantastic save that not only kept his team in the game but also sent a message to the other team: this match wasn't just about strength; it was also about brains.

Lehmann's approach reminds us that in any field—be it sports, school, or the arts—preparation is crucial. Young readers should recognize that while talent is great, real excellence often springs from the effort you put in when no one is watching. It's about those late-night study sessions, the many hours spent practicing, and being open to learning from others. This is what Lehmann exemplified—dedication and determination rooted in thorough preparation.

Soccer can be unpredictable, but thanks to Lehmann's preparation, he managed to turn that unpredictability into a game of strategy. He made his opponents second-guess their instincts. Just imagine standing at the penalty spot, feeling the weight of the moment, knowing that the goalkeeper has carefully studied your every move. That's a mental edge that few possess.

Lehmann's path wasn't without challenges. There were times when his preparation didn't lead to the results he wanted. Sometimes, the ball would find the back of the net despite his best efforts, and that's part of the game. However, it was his unyielding spirit that drove him to analyze those moments too. What went wrong? How could he improve? In those times of reflection, he gained insights that strengthened his approach for the future. This resilience is another important lesson for young athletes: failure isn't the end; it's a chance to grow.

What Lehmann did so well was to embrace the idea that every challenge, every setback, was a chance to learn. Young readers can take a page from his story and apply this mindset to their lives, whether it's on the soccer field, in the classroom, or in their hobbies. Instead of shying away from difficult situations, they can face them head-on, equipped with knowledge and a plan.

So, the next time you find yourself on the field or in the classroom, remember Jens Lehmann's example. Bring your own homework. Be prepared. Analyze, learn, and strategize. You might discover that your own preparation can be your secret weapon, leading you to victories and accomplishments you once thought were beyond your reach. Whether you're an aspiring soccer player or a student dedicated to a project, the truth remains the same: hard work truly pays off, and often, it's the key that opens the door to success.

Mind Games on the Field

When the whistle blew and the weight of the moment settled in, it was Jens Lehmann's time to shine. Penalty shootouts, where luck and skill often tangled in a tense dance, were his playground. The crowd held its breath, leaning forward in their seats as if their collective hopes could sway the outcome.

But Lehmann found his own rhythm. For him, it was a mental game, a chess match played in a high-pressure arena, and he was ready to step into the shoes of the clever strategist.

Imagine being a young player standing at the penalty spot, your heart pounding like a drum, nervously glancing at the towering figure in goal. You're about to kick the ball that could bring glory to your team or send everyone into despair. Now picture that goalkeeper, sporting something unexpected: notes tucked into his socks. That's right! Lehmann's quirky tactic wasn't just for show; it was a brilliant psychological move. As he pulled out those neatly penned notes, the atmosphere shifted. The tension on the field was so thick you could almost cut it with a knife, and those notes were a clear reminder to everyone watching—this goalkeeper was no ordinary player; he had done his homework.

Envision the scene: an opposing player stands ready, prepared to take his shot. He's trained tirelessly for this moment, but as he looks at Lehmann, unease washes over him. This goalkeeper is more than just a barrier; he's a strategist. Lehmann's careful planning turned him into a figure of unpredictability. The players now faced a double challenge: not only did they have to score, but they also had to navigate the mind games playing out before them. It was no longer just about making the kick; it was about facing the boldness of a goalkeeper who dared to outsmart them.

"Is he really pulling out notes from his socks?" one player might think in disbelief, as doubt crept in. That mental edge was just as vital as any physical advantage on the field. Lehmann's antics weren't merely a reflection of his personality; they were tools in his toolkit that blurred the line between confidence and intimidation. For young athletes, this offers an important lesson: success often comes from thinking outside the box when facing challenges.

In these high-stakes moments, the atmosphere grew electric. The sounds of the cheering crowd faded away, replaced by the rhythmic beating of a thousand hearts, all their hopes hanging in the balance. Lehmann thrived in this intensity, like a maestro conducting a symphony of pressure and expectation. The brighter the spotlight, the more he dazzled. He could sense the apprehension radiating from the shooter, a feeling that was both palpable and contagious. Lehmann turned that fear into fuel for his own determination.

A funny story highlights this perfectly. In one unforgettable match, as the opposition geared up for their first penalty kick, Lehmann decided to shake things up a bit. When the player stepped forward, ready to take the shot,

Lehmann dramatically pulled out his notes from his socks, flipping through them with exaggerated flair. The look on the shooter's face was priceless—a mix of confusion and disbelief. It was as if Lehmann had just opened a secret file filled with all the player's most embarrassing kicking secrets. While all this was in good fun, it clearly demonstrated how Lehmann used humor as a psychological weapon, catching his opponents off guard just before their crucial moment.

But humor wasn't the only card Lehmann played. He was also a sharp observer of human behavior. Each penalty shootout revealed unique patterns and tendencies from the shooters, and he was quick to seize those insights. He studied not only their kicking styles but also their body language, their breathing, and how they positioned themselves. He could sense when they were anxious, overly confident, or completely determined. This deep understanding of psychology allowed him to create an environment where the pressure became a burden for his opponents, while it felt thrilling for him.

Consider his encounter with a particularly skilled forward known for powerful penalties. The player was famous for his accuracy, and everyone in the stadium believed he was destined to score. But Lehmann had a plan. As the player approached the penalty spot, Lehmann confidently positioned himself, refusing to back down and instead narrowing his focus. When the whistle blew, Lehmann stayed still, exuding a calm confidence that could be as intimidating as any show of aggression.

What happened next was both surprising and a testament to Lehmann's careful preparation. As the player wound up, he hesitated for just a split second, caught off guard by Lehmann's unwavering presence. That tiny moment was all it took for Lehmann to spring into action, diving with the grace of an acrobat and deflecting the ball away from the net. The crowd erupted into thunderous cheers, but it was the look of disbelief on the shooter's face that told the true story: Lehmann had not only saved a goal; he had outsmarted a formidable opponent.

This was more than just a game; it was a captivating dance of mind and body, strategy and execution. And at the heart of it all was Lehmann, armed with his secret notes and a firm belief in his abilities. Young readers should pay attention: every moment of pressure is a chance to shine, not just for those who are naturally gifted, but for those who are clever, prepared, and strategic.

The mental battles of the penalty shootout are something many young players might not fully understand. But think of it this way: every time you step onto the field—whether it's for practice or a crucial match—you're facing not just your opponents but also the weight of expectations. Lehmann's story reminds us that preparation is key, but so is the ability to think creatively when the stakes are high.

Young athletes can learn to embrace pressure instead of shying away from it. There's real power in knowing you have the skills to turn things in your favor. The next time you find yourself in a tense situation, whether on the soccer field, in class, or in any other challenge, remember that confidence and preparation are your best friends.

Just like Lehmann used the little details of the game to throw his opponents off their rhythm, young readers can find their own unique ways to tackle challenges. You don't need to be the fastest or the strongest; sometimes, a sharp mind and a touch of humor can create all the difference. Who knows? Your own "sock notes" might lead you to your greatest successes.

So, as you lace up your cleats for your next match or dive into that tough school project, channel your inner Jens Lehmann. Carry with you the understanding that preparation and creativity go hand in hand. Remember, it's not just about scoring goals or achieving grades; it's about the journey, the lessons learned, and the excitement of the challenge. In the grand scheme of life, every moment of pressure is just another opportunity to shine, laugh, and outsmart the odds.

Triumph Through Tactics

Winning on the soccer field isn't just about having the best skills or sheer strength; it's a mix of strategy, preparation, and a little bit of luck. Jens Lehmann perfectly demonstrated this idea, turning the simple act of saving penalties into a brilliant display of tactical thinking. Imagine this: a crucial match where the score is tight, and the pressure could decide the game. This is where Lehmann truly excelled—not just as a goalkeeper but as a clever strategist who knew how to use his skills with amazing finesse.

One of the standout moments of his career happened during the 2006 FIFA World Cup quarter-finals, a match that became a legendary showcase of Lehmann's talent. As the crowd buzzed with excitement, Lehmann geared up for a potential penalty shootout against Argentina—an impressive team filled with players known for their accuracy and calmness under stress. But Lehmann, always composed, had put in the work to prepare. He didn't just study the players; he took note of their tendencies, their nervous habits, and the moments they might falter.

When the moment arrived, the atmosphere was electric. Lehmann thrived in this pressure, standing confidently on the goal line, almost challenging the shooters to take their best shot. This wasn't just about blocking the ball; it was a game of wits. As the first Argentine player stepped up, you could sense the weight of expectation pressing down on everyone. Lehmann's mind was racing with calculations, recalling the notes he'd made about the player's past penalty kicks.

The whistle blew, and the world held its breath. The player hit the ball hard, but Lehmann was ready. He leaped with his arms stretched wide, and with a stunning dive, he made the save! The crowd erupted in cheers, marking the start of a fantastic display where Lehmann's strategic brilliance shone even more brightly.

What really set Lehmann apart wasn't just his physical skills but also his understanding of the psychological side of the game. Each penalty save reflected his careful preparation and tactical savvy, turning pressure into a thrilling advantage. As the next Argentine players approached, each feeling the weight of their nerves, Lehmann stood as a solid wall.

One particularly intense moment came when Lehmann faced one of Argentina's most talented forwards, known for his cool demeanor and ability to place the ball exactly where he wanted. As the forward came closer, fully focused, Lehmann locked eyes with him. With a playful grin, he briefly glanced at the stands, as if something fascinating was happening there. That small distraction was enough to shake the forward's concentration for just a moment.

The ball was kicked, but Lehmann dove the other way—only to recover just in time and reach out to deflect the shot. It was pure magic! The ball bounced away, and the stadium exploded in cheers. This was more than just a save; it was a well-timed gamble that paid off. Lehmann's clever antics showed how a simple distraction could change the game, not just for that moment but throughout the entire match.

As the shootout continued, Lehmann's confidence grew. With each save, he lifted not only his own spirits but those of his teammates. The mental battle of the shootout had shifted in his favor. Every penalty kick became a reflection of the ongoing struggle on the field— an exciting blend of skill, mental toughness, and unwavering determination. His strategic approach reinforced the idea that preparation could be as powerful as physical talent.

But let's not forget the thrill that comes with these defining moments. Penalty shootouts are famously unpredictable, yet Lehmann always found ways to prepare for that uncertainty. He would spend hours watching footage of opposing players, studying their patterns and habits. He understood that knowledge was his greatest weapon, helping him to predict what might happen next. This meticulous attention to detail kept him one step ahead, turning each penalty kick into a chance for victory.

And if you think this only applies to soccer, think again! The core of Lehmann's strategy can be applied to many challenges in life. Whether you're getting ready for a big exam, trying to impress during a presentation, or preparing for a competitive tryout, remember that being prepared can help you think strategically. Just like Lehmann, young readers can create their own game plans and tactical advantages in everyday situations.

Imagine a young athlete, nerves tingling before a crucial penalty shootout in a big match, recalling the strategies learned from Lehmann's story. Instead of feeling overwhelmed, they could turn that energy into positive thinking. They might even jot down their own "notes" to help them focus on their strengths. Just as Lehmann used humor and creativity to gain an edge, young people can discover their own ways to face challenges head-on.

Lehmann's legendary saves didn't come from raw talent alone; they were the result of countless hours of practice, preparation, and thoughtful strategy. A kid watching from the sidelines could learn that being a hero isn't just about accolades. It's about understanding the game, playing smart, and embracing the excitement of the challenge.

One of the most inspiring parts of Lehmann's journey is how he continued to adapt and learn from each experience. Every match, every save, every missed shot from an opponent—these weren't just numbers on a scoreboard; they were lessons that contributed to his mastery. Young readers, pay attention: every setback or challenge is a chance to refine your strategy and boost your skills. Just as Lehmann adjusted his tactics during tough moments, you too can learn to navigate life's unexpected twists and turns.

So, the next time you face a daunting challenge, think of Lehmann and his amazing saves. Embrace your unique strengths, learn from those who've been there before you, and don't hesitate to think outside the box. Like Lehmann, you might discover that creativity, strategy, and preparation can be your greatest allies.

As the final whistle blew in that unforgettable World Cup match, and Lehmann celebrated his victory with his teammates, it was more than just a win on the scoreboard; it was a triumph for strategic thinking and mental resilience. And in that moment, every young player watching learned a simple yet profound lesson: success comes from being smart, ready, and brave.

Embrace your own unique strategies in life, whether they involve soccer, school, or any other passion. Remember, every moment on the field, in the classroom, or anywhere else is a chance to save the day—just like Jens Lehmann did countless times throughout his incredible career. Take that leap, dive into the unknown, and you just might surprise yourself with what you achieve. You might not need to pull notes from your socks, but you will definitely leave your mark by facing every challenge with the heart of a champion.

Chapter 10: Samba Magic: Neymar's Joyful Play

Streets to Stardom

For Neymar da Silva Santos Júnior, the streets of Mogi das Cruzes, Brazil, were more than just a playground; they were the stage where he started to create his story of success. This tale calls out from the lively alleys of Brazil, where every dribble, every kick, and every playful dance with the ball formed a note in a melody that would eventually echo across the globe.

Born on February 5, 1992, Neymar grew up in a place buzzing with football passion. The sport was deeply woven into the fabric of his family and community. His father, a skilled player himself, spotted the spark of talent in young Neymar and nurtured it with encouragement and support. In this lively environment, filled with laughter and the joyful shouts of kids chasing their dreams, Neymar began to dream his own—dreams that would one day propel him onto the world stage.

Imagine the sun setting over the dusty streets, casting a warm golden glow on makeshift goals made from sticks. Children gathered, barefoot and full of joy, crafting stories of glory with every flick of the ball. Neymar, with his wild hair and contagious smile, stood at the center of it all. To him, these streets weren't just paths; they were arenas. Each game was like a mini World Cup, every opponent a stepping stone, and each goal scored a glimpse of a bright future.

But while the joyful chaos of neighborhood games lit up Neymar's spirit, there were also challenges lurking in the background. The da Silva family faced financial struggles that threatened to dim Neymar's growing talent. With his father bringing in a modest income and daily expenses on the rise, there were days when dreams felt heavy and far away. Yet, challenges often build resilience, and for Neymar, it was an early lesson in meeting hardship with determination. He learned to appreciate the small moments—like dribbling a ball alongside friends who shared not just the joys of the game but also life's difficulties.

The desire to rise above his situation ignited a fierce determination within him. Neymar hit the streets with an energy that many could only admire. His days were filled with hours of practice, often perfecting his skills long after the sun had set. The concrete served as his training ground, with neighborhood kids becoming his unyielding rivals. In this small world of soccer, Neymar discovered the art of improvisation, a quality that would later define his unique playing style.

His creativity bloomed like wildflowers in a concrete jungle. As the ball danced at his feet, he tried out moves inspired by the professional players he idolized. He practiced flicks, tricks, and feints, weaving through imaginary defenders with a flair that brought gasps and cheers from his friends. The streets rang with the sounds of excitement and disappointment as Neymar repeatedly tried and stumbled, only to get back up with an unbreakable spirit. Each fall was a lesson, each setback a chance to rise with even more determination.

The rhythm of those street soccer matches was exhilarating; they were more than just games; they were grand events filled with passion, laughter, and even tears. Neymar's heart raced with excitement as he danced through makeshift defenses. In those moments, he wasn't just a kid playing a game; he was an artist creating a masterpiece with every touch of the ball. His imagination turned the ordinary into something magical, transforming simple matches into a beautiful display of skill and creativity.

As he continued to impress with his talent, whispers began to spread. The boy who could seemingly float with the ball was starting to catch the eye of local coaches. Neymar's relentless pursuit of excellence opened doors he never thought he could access. But the stakes were high; talent alone wouldn't be enough. The pressure to perform grew as he transitioned from casual games to organized competitions.

Each match became a test, not just of skill but of character. As a young boy with dreams soaring high, Neymar faced the reality that success often comes with expectations. He experienced setbacks and moments of doubt when the pressure felt overwhelming. Yet, during those tough times, he remembered the joy of playing in the streets, the simplicity of running free, and enjoying every moment on the field. This served as a reminder that the heart of soccer lies not only in victory but in the joy of the game itself.

Neymar's early years can be seen as a masterclass in perseverance. Each time he laced up his worn-out sneakers, he prepared not just for a game but for the lessons that lay ahead. He learned about teamwork and friendship, building bonds that would last a lifetime. The thrill of celebrating a hard-earned victory with teammates became sweeter with each shared experience.

Moreover, these moments instilled a deep sense of humility. As the young prodigy climbed higher, he stayed grounded by the love and support of his family and community. Neymar's rise was a collective journey, with every goal reflecting the sacrifices and dedication of those who believed in him. He never forgot where he came from, often recalling how the laughter of friends resonated louder than the cheers of stadium crowds.

While the streets shaped Neymar into a soccer superstar, they also served as a classroom for vital life lessons. He learned that success isn't achieved overnight; it's built through consistent effort and a willingness to adapt. He came to understand that failure is not a dead end but a stepping stone on the road to greatness. And perhaps most importantly, he realized that the heart of the game lies not just in the scoreboard but in the connections forged both on and off the field.

As Neymar moved from the streets to the first steps of professional soccer, he carried with him the spirit of those carefree days spent playing with friends. Those memories became a source of inspiration, fueling his desire to express himself through his craft—an expression that would captivate millions around the world.

This colorful journey from the streets of Brazil to the bright lights of stadiums worldwide is not just a story of victory; it's a powerful reminder that the dreams of a child, driven by passion and hard work, can truly soar. Neymar's tale encourages young readers to look beyond the obstacles they may face, urging them to pursue their dreams with the same enthusiasm that ignited a boy's hopes in the streets of Mogi das Cruzes. It shows that each dribble, every goal, and every moment spent doing what they love is a step toward their own unique journey.

The path may be filled with challenges, but with dedication and creativity, they too can turn their dreams into reality. The streets may have been where it all began, but the world is vast, and the future shines brightly for those who dare to believe.

The Art of the Game

When Neymar steps onto the soccer field, it feels like the world stops to watch a true artist at work. He brings a spark to the game that's both exciting and contagious. Every time he gets the ball, fans hold their breath, wondering what magical moment he will create next. Neymar plays with a flair that celebrates imagination, using signature moves that mesmerize audiences and leave defenders in a state of confusion.

One of Neymar's most famous moves is the daring "rainbow flick." This trick involves flicking the ball over his head and behind his back, often leaving opponents scratching their heads in disbelief. It's a display of creativity and confidence that Neymar has mastered to perfection. Picture this: during an early match with Santos, defenders were closing in on him, but instead of panicking, Neymar seized the moment. He executed the rainbow flick with incredible skill, sending the ball soaring over one defender and zipping past another who was left stunned. The crowd erupted in cheers, completely captivated by his talent. That moment truly captured Neymar's essence— joyful, bold, and one of a kind.

But Neymar's artistry doesn't stop with flashy tricks. His playing style combines skill, quick footwork, and genuine joy. He dances with the ball, spinning around defenders with a playful grin that shows he's having the time of his life. It's as if he's a kid playing in the streets, free from the pressures that often come with professional sports. For Neymar, soccer is more than just a game; it's a way to express himself.

So, what can young players learn from Neymar's approach? At the core of his style is the idea of being true to oneself. Instead of trying to fit into a mold, Neymar inspires aspiring soccer stars to embrace their unique talents and let their personalities shine on the field. Just like every artist has a different way of painting, every player has their own unique style. It's all about trying new moves and finding joy in the game, rather than only focusing on winning.

Imagine a young player named Liam, standing on the field and hesitating to try a trick he picked up from watching Neymar. He might be worried about looking silly or making a mistake. This is where Neymar's spirit comes into play. To be creative, you need to let go of the fear of failure. Neymar didn't become a superstar by playing it safe. He practiced tirelessly, took risks, and faced setbacks, but always bounced back. Every mistake was just another step on his journey to greatness.

It's important to remember that the art of soccer isn't just about the fancy tricks. It's also about the rhythm and flow of the game. Neymar has a natural ability to read the field, anticipating plays and reacting without hesitation. His footwork resembles a dance—quick, smooth, and elegant. He moves across the field as if he's having a conversation with the ball, understanding it in a way that few can. Young players should keep in mind that playing isn't just about perfect technique; it's about feeling the rhythm of the game, the excitement of the crowd, and the energy of their teammates.

Think back to a sunny day at the park, where kids gather for a spontaneous soccer game. Players of all ages form teams, and the excitement fills the air. On this day, young Liam decides to channel his inner Neymar. As he dribbles the ball down the field, he spots his friend Matt waiting for a pass. Without overthinking, Liam remembers the rainbow flick he saw Neymar do, and he gives it a go. The ball sails over his head and lands perfectly at Matt's feet, who, surprised but delighted, runs forward to score. That spontaneous moment reminds us that creativity thrives when we're having fun and supporting one another.

Furthermore, soccer is not just about individual skill; it's also about connection and teamwork. Neymar has always shown how vital it is to work well with teammates. His talent for making perfect passes or assisting in brilliant plays highlights the importance of collaboration in achieving success. In soccer, every player contributes to a bigger picture, creating a melody that resonates on the field. Young players should focus on building strong relationships with their teammates, learning to communicate and recognize each other's strengths. When they create harmony on the field, they elevate not only their own performance but the game as a whole.

Let's take a moment to appreciate soccer from a different perspective. Picture a local team practicing on a cool evening, filled with laughter and excitement. Each player isn't just trying to get better at their skills; they are weaving together a shared story. It's during these moments of passion and teamwork that real magic happens. The thrill of a perfectly timed pass, the satisfaction of executing a well-planned play, and the joy of celebrating a goal together make the game truly special. Just as Neymar learned from his early days in the streets, it's about finding joy in every moment and appreciating the journey just as much as the outcome.

A memorable story from Neymar's career illustrates this spirit perfectly. During a challenging match, the opposing team had their defenses locked tight, making it tough to break through. Nevertheless, Neymar didn't give up; he kept dribbling and maneuvering around defenders as if he were painting a masterpiece. Suddenly, he saw a teammate making a run for the goal. With a swift flick of his wrist, he sent a perfectly timed pass flying through the air. The teammate caught it effortlessly and scored a stunning goal. The crowd went wild, and for Neymar, it was a reminder that creativity benefits not just the individual but the whole team.

Being creative in sports isn't just about putting on a show for the fans; it's about the experiences, the joy, and the memories built along the way. Every player has their own story, and their unique contributions make the game richer and more exciting. Whether a young player is trying out their first trick or refining their skills, they should remember that every practice session, every friendly match, and every challenge on the field shapes their personal narrative.

With this in mind, Neymar shines as a motivating example for young athletes everywhere. He shows them that soccer is an extension of their identities—a canvas where they can express their dreams. So, as they step onto the field, they should do so with open hearts and a desire to express themselves. The game is a playground, a stage, and a community where everyone's contributions add to the overall experience of soccer. It's about daring to try new things, embracing mistakes, and enjoying every goal scored and every friendship made. In this beautiful blend of life and sport, every player adds their unique note to the greater melody, and the world is excited to hear their story.

A Goal for the Ages

The atmosphere in the stadium buzzed with excitement, a vibrant energy that seemed to fill the air all around. This was a crucial match, a moment that would be remembered by every fan who had come to witness it. As the sun dipped low, casting a warm glow over the field, the packed stands roared with anticipation. It was one of those special evenings where dreams could come true and legends could be made, a night where every heartbeat echoed the hope of supporters who had traveled from near and far to cheer on their heroes.

When the whistle blew to kick off the match, Neymar stepped onto the field radiating determination. Just his presence alone sent the crowd into a frenzy. Fans proudly donned his jersey, waving flags and chanting his name. They believed in him, and he could feel their expectations buzzing around him like electricity. As the ball was set in motion, it was clear that Neymar was in his element. He glided across the field with a grace that felt almost magical, every touch intentional, every movement a dance that left defenders confused and off-balance.

The match unfolded like a captivating story. Both teams fought fiercely for control, trading blows with precision. The crowd erupted at every close call, every slick pass, and every incredible save. Yet, Neymar was determined to leave his mark. With every touch, he carved a path through the opposing players, pushing forward with an unquenchable thirst for victory. The tension in the stadium grew thicker; fans leaned forward in their seats, hearts racing with hope and excitement.

As the minutes ticked by, the game dragged on with no goals in sight. Pressure mounted; every play seemed to carry the weight of expectations. Neymar felt it. He had faced challenges before, but this felt different. Taking a deep breath, he recalled the countless hours spent practicing back in São Paulo. Each dribble, flick of the ball, and goal scored in his youth echoed in his mind. He knew this was his moment, a chance to change the game, to inspire and unite everyone who believed in him.

Then came the moment that would forever be etched in the hearts of fans everywhere. A break in play opened a window of opportunity as Neymar received a pass from a teammate. He gathered the ball, his eyes scanning the field like a hawk. Time seemed to slow down as he weighed his options. To his right, a defender closed in; to his left, another lurked, ready to pounce. But Neymar had a plan. With a light touch, he pulled the ball closer, inviting the challenge, teasing his opponents.

In an instant, he executed a stunning move, blending his signature flair with the tenacity of a true athlete. He faked left, making it seem like he would sprint that way, only to spin back to the right, leaving the defenders grasping at nothing but air. The stadium erupted in a chorus of gasps and cheers as he zipped past the dazed players, a flash of yellow and green in the eyes of his adoring fans.

As he approached the penalty area, the goalkeeper shifted nervously, preparing to cut down the distance. Neymar's heart raced, but he kept his cool. He was no stranger to pressure. Taking one more touch to set himself up perfectly, he launched a powerful shot. The ball soared through the air, an arc of hope and ambition, as the crowd held its breath.

Time stood still as the ball raced toward the goal, the keeper diving with all his strength, arms reaching out in a desperate attempt to stop it. But Neymar's shot was too accurate, too forceful. It hit the back of the net with a loud thud that sent shockwaves of joy rolling through the stadium. The crowd erupted into a symphony of cheers, a wave of sound that swept across the arena, drowning everything else in a moment of pure elation.

In that moment, Neymar became more than just a player; he was a hero, a symbol of resilience, creativity, and the unbreakable spirit of the game. He sprinted toward the corner flag, arms raised in celebration, a huge smile lighting up his face. The adrenaline rush and sheer joy of the moment took over him. He had not just scored a goal; he had given his team and their supporters a memory that would last a lifetime.

Later on, as Neymar reflected on that incredible goal, he often spoke about the mix of feelings that flooded through him. "It wasn't just about scoring; it was about the bond with the fans, the joy of being part of something bigger than myself," he would say, his eyes shining with the memory. He understood that each goal, every moment on the field, carried the weight of his journey, a tribute to the countless hours of practice and the unwavering belief that had driven him to that stage.

That night, as the echoes of celebration faded into the twilight, it became clear that this moment was not just a highlight in Neymar's career; it was a message for aspiring players everywhere. It captured the essence of what it means to chase dreams, to confront challenges head-on, and to celebrate the beauty of the game. For every young athlete watching, it was a call to dream big and practice hard.

The road to that goal wasn't always smooth. Neymar faced setbacks and moments of self-doubt, but each challenge only strengthened his determination. "I learned early on that resilience is crucial. There were times I stumbled, when I felt like giving up, but I understood that every setback was just a step on my journey," he would often share with young fans who admired him.

This truth resonates deeply; greatness is often shaped by adversity. For Neymar, those late nights on the practice field, the tough training sessions, and the sacrifices made were all part of the journey that led to that unforgettable moment. It served as a lesson in perseverance, a boost for anyone who might hesitate or doubt themselves. Each goal scored, each trick perfected, and every ounce of passion put into the game would eventually pay off in ways they could only start to envision.

The thrill of the game, the joy of expressing himself through soccer, and the connections forged with teammates were all vital to his success. Neymar believed in the power of connection, both with the ball and with the fans cheering for him. "When you play with love and joy, you invite others to join you. That's what soccer is all about," he said. His journey wasn't just a personal victory; it was an invitation for young players to find their own way, to embrace their unique skills, and to share their love for the game.

As the night stretched on, and the celebrations continued, Neymar's goal turned into more than just a moment; it sparked inspiration. It ignited a fire in the hearts of countless young athletes, motivating them to pursue their own dreams with passion and commitment. With every practice session, they could aim to create their own unforgettable moments, moments that would echo through the years.

Neymar's journey teaches us that every great player starts somewhere, often with humble beginnings and a dream. Young athletes, just like him, should grab every chance to sharpen their skills, express their individuality, and connect with their teammates. It's about more than just winning;

it's about the experiences, the growth, and the memories created along the way.

The story of that goal serves as a guiding light for aspiring soccer stars, a reminder that success is within reach for those willing to put in the hard work and embrace who they really are. So, as they lace up their boots and step onto the field, they should carry with them the spirit of that moment—a moment filled with joy, determination, and the belief that they too can make their dreams come true. With every kick, every goal, and every game played, they can write their own story, adding their unique chapter to the beautiful game of soccer.

References

Chapter 1:
Cristiano Ronaldo's journey from poverty to world's biggest sports star: https://www.standardmedia.co.ke/entertainment/news/article/2001342412/cristiano-ronaldos-journey-from-poverty-to-worlds-biggest-sports-star

Cristiano Ronaldo: How He Grew Up - The Mast: https://mastmedia.plu.edu/2024/special-feature-by-kids-2/

The Tiger Mentality: How Cristiano Ronaldo's Work Ethic Has Helped Him Achieve Greatness: https://4pballer.com/the-tiger-mentality-how-cristiano-ronaldos-work-ethic-has-helped-him-achieve-greatness/

Chapter 2:
Lionel Messi - Wikipedia: https://en.wikipedia.org/wiki/Messi

Lionel Messi | Records, Height, Ballon d'Or, Inter Miami, & Facts: https://www.britannica.com/biography/Lionel-Messi

Chapter 3:
Alex Morgan - Wikipedia:
https://en.wikipedia.org/wiki/Alex_Morgan

Alex Morgan | Biography, Titles, & Facts:
https://www.britannica.com/biography/Alex-Morgan

Chapter 4:
Pelé - Biography, 3x World Cup Champion, Brazilian Soccer Player:
https://www.biography.com/athletes/pele

Pelé - life and legacy - Football history:
https://www.footballhistory.org/player/pele.html

Chapter 5:
Total Football - Wikipedia:
https://en.wikipedia.org/wiki/Total_Football

How Johan Cruyff shaped Ajax, Barcelona, world soccer - ESPN:
https://www.espn.com/soccer/story/_/id/37615433/how-shaped-ajax-barcelona-world-soccer

Chapter 6:
'The Miracle of Istanbul': When Liverpool Pulled Off the Greatest ...:

https://www.givemesport.com/liverpool-2005-champions-league-istanbul/

What was the Miracle of Istanbul? Liverpool's 2005 Champions ...: https://www.goal.com/en-us/news/what-was-the-miracle-of-istanbul-liverpools-2005-champions-league-final-comeback-explained/lytj7tlcrpnz1aop3a35qn9w1

2005 UEFA Champions League final - Wikipedia: https://en.wikipedia.org/wiki/2005_UEFA_Champions_League_final

Chapter 7:
Pele recounts Gordon Banks' 1970 World Cup save in moving tribute: https://www.skysports.com/football/news/12027/11635417/pele-recounts-gordon-banks-1970-world-cup-save-in-moving-tribute

Gordon Banks saves from Pelé in world cup 1970 - YouTube: https://www.youtube.com/watch?v=pei-2wPJS2o

Chapter 8:
Kylian Mbappe Biography, Career Info, Records & Achievements:

https://www.sportskeeda.com/player/kylian-mbappe

Kylian Mbappe | Biography & Facts - Britannica: https://www.britannica.com/biography/Kylian-Mbappe

Kylian Mbappé to donate all his World Cup winnings to children's ...: https://www.riglobal.org/kylian-mbappe-to-donate-all-his-world-cup-winnings-to-childrens-charity/

Chapter 9:
Lehmann's World Cup penalty note fetches one million euros | Reuters: https://www.reuters.com/article/sports/soccer/lehmann-world-cup-penalty-note-fetches-one-million-euros-idUSL16853757/Germany in Semi-Final After Penalty Drama Against Argentina - DW: https://www.dw.com/en/germany-in-semi-final-after-penalty-drama-against-argentina/a-2074644Lehmann gets help against Argentina penalty takers - ESPN: http://www.espn.com/general/story?id=2506652&src=desktop

Chapter 10:
Neymar | Biography & Facts -

Britannica: https://www.britannica.com/biography/NeymarNeymar: Biography, Brazilian Soccer Player,

Athlete: https://www.biography.com/athletes/neymarNeymar -

Wikipedia: https://en.wikipedia.org/wiki/Neymar

W. Bo Cricklewood

Made in United States
Cleveland, OH
04 August 2025